The Eulogy of Pittsburgh's Schenley Spartans

Mark Hostutler

Published by BookLocker.com, Inc., Bradenton, Florida.

Printed in the United States of America on acid-free paper.

BookLocker.com, Inc.
2015

First Edition

For the only two Holdens I know.

You both inspire me.

"The trouble with the rat race is that even if you win, you're still a rat."

—Minister William Sloane Coffin Jr.
Riverside Church, New York City
July 29, 1979

About the Author

Mark Hostutler is a former award-winning journalist at the *Delaware County Times* and the author of *Heads of State: Pennsylvania's Greatest High School Basketball Players of the Modern Era*, a book that profiles the best scholastic players in the Keystone State's illustrious history. His work has also appeared in *SLAM Magazine* and the *Basketball Times*. A resident of West Chester, Hostutler now teaches English and Sports Literature at Coatesville High School, his alma mater. He earned his bachelor's degree in communications from Elizabethtown College and his master's degree in English from West Chester University. To contact him, e-mail guruhoss@yahoo.com.

Contents

I. The Rat Race

DURING THE **21**ST CENTURY, high school basketball—specifically in and around America's urban settings—has devolved into an arms race akin to what has been transpiring on the college level for decades. The rat race of Division I hoops has turned coaches into caricatures of used-car salesmen, equipped with all the unsavory recruiting tactics that reinforce every negative stereotype associated with the profession.

And since we all know what flows downhill, the scholastic ranks, supposedly the last bastion of amateurism and integrity, have gradually become the bastardized offspring of college basketball.

Charter schools and prep schools, private schools and cyber schools. These alternative approaches to education, while valuable in their own unique ways, have torn at the fabric of high school sports, especially basketball. The game's five-on-five nature enables programs to quickly build something out of nothing, since it only takes a handful of great players for a team to become championship-worthy.

As a result, the nation's best prospects are poached and rarely represent the communities that nurtured their development. Before high school games are even contested on the floor, they are done so in a high-stakes marketplace where teenagers, some not far removed from puberty, are lured away from their neighborhoods through the promise of a better future. That's how the likes of Rod Strickland, Ron Mercer, Rajon Rondo, Josh Smith, and Brandon Jennings—natives of New York, Tennessee, Kentucky, Georgia, and California, respectively—flock to Mouth of Wilson, Virginia, hundreds of miles from home. If not for basketball, no one outside the region would even know that Oak Hill Academy—a 150-student boarding school in the Appalachian Mountains, near the North Carolina border— even exists. However, the powerhouse program, which also counts Carmelo Anthony and Jerry Stackhouse among its graduates, is nationally renowned, having finished No. 1 or 2 in the *USA Today* scholastic rankings 14 times since 1990.

> These alternative approaches to education have torn at the fabric of high school sports.

Findlay Prep, a high school basketball team without a high school, is another hoops factory, and one that isn't shy about its mission. The team's dozen players are Findlay Prep's only students, and they take classes at a separate private school across the street from their five-bedroom, four-bathroom house in Henderson, Nevada.

In Southeastern Pennsylvania, the tiny American Christian School in Aston Township opened its doors to high school students in the early 1990s, and it remained relatively unknown even to county residents until a fledgling star decided to enroll. And when he left, the school ceased to exist. Tyreke Evans—from Chester, the hoops-obsessed city that borders Aston—attended American Christian so he could begin his high school career in seventh grade. By his 11th-grade year, Reebok had won a bidding war to outfit his team, which resembled more of an AAU club than a scholastic one, as it barnstormed the country. They played almost 40 games, some of which were the college length of 40 minutes. Amidst criticism that the school, which operated out of a Baptist church and adjacent trailers, was a diploma mill and a vehicle for Evans, it survived not even one week without him. American Christian closed up shop days after Evans departed for the University of Memphis to embark on a journey that saw him become the 2010 NBA Rookie of the Year.

This, of course, shouldn't be too much of an issue for people who hold the nostalgic view of scholastic sports being my town versus your town. Oak Hill, Findlay, and American Christian, after all, are or were independent of the Virginia High School League, Nevada Interscholastic Activities Association, and Pennsylvania Interscholastic Athletic Association. Therefore, they cannot or could not prevent public schools, which are subjected to a different set of rules, from bagging state titles. Furthermore, it's acceptable when a kid finds a school that can facilitate his growth better than the one in his zip code.

It becomes problematic, however, when programs of their ilk are permitted to vie for state supremacy alongside John Q. Public High School. For example, the PIAA, the Keystone State's governing body of high school sports, allows almost every high school in the commonwealth's 46,000 square miles to contend for state-championship hardware. That includes charter schools comprised of students who spend more time in commute than in class, and Catholic schools that suit up ringers who won't be found in the communion line on Sundays.

Consider the charter school movement in Philadelphia that has completely altered the PIAA terrain. The school district's perennially dire financial straits—coupled with its label as a failure, according to the criteria of the No Child Left Behind Act of 2001—have ushered in an era of not only educational but athletic upheaval. (Charter schools have been draining resources from the cash-strapped city for so long that the 2013-2014 school year began with a $304 million deficit that forced the distribution of more than 4,000 pink slips to teachers, principals, and other support staff.)

Philadelphia's tidal wave of change on the hardwood began to swell during the winter of 2001-02, when the Prep Charter basketball team became the first of a staggering number of charter schools that now compete on the varsity level. That season, the Huskies, as expected, were punching bags with a 3-16 record and suffered a pair of losses, 66-16 and 109-60. Four years later, Prep Charter, aided by the interior presence of twin forwards Marcus and Markieff Morris, earned the first of back-to-back state championships (Class 2A) with a 31-point blowout in the title game. The current members of the Phoenix Suns had engineered quite a turnaround for a school that was converted from a vacant supermarket.

All of these factors make what the Schenley High School basketball team achieved on the other side of the commonwealth during the 2006-07 season even more extraordinary. The players grew up within a stone's throw of one another in the same hard-knock neighborhood in Pittsburgh, and had known each other since their first days dribbling a ball.

II. The Heyday of Western Pennsylvania Basketball

SURELY, NOT MANY SPORTS FANS would ever confuse the Pittsburgh area's history of generating blue-chip ballers with that of Philadelphia, which churns out talent like it does cheese steaks—with assembly-line efficiency. (Earl Monroe, Kobe Bryant, Tom Gola, Rasheed Wallace, and Wilt Chamberlain—all City of Brotherly Love natives—would be a formidable starting five, to say the least.) However, the Steel City and its suburbs once tantalized mobs of eager college coaches, particularly during the countercultural years of the 1960s and '70s.

"Pittsburgh was once one of the most fertile recruiting grounds in the country," said Sonny Vaccaro, the slick-talking czar of grassroots basketball who turned summer hoops into a multimillion-dollar industry. The 75-year-old former marketing executive built the brands of Nike, Adidas, and Reebok by putting their sneakers on the best players in the world, from preps to pros. "I grew up right outside the city [in Trafford], and saw first-hand the talent in the area."

In 1965, Vaccaro, then in his mid-20s, created the Dapper Dan Roundball Classic in his backyard. It was the nation's first scholastic All-Star game, and it pitted Pennsylvania's best against the rest of America's and annually packed the 17,000-seat Civic Arena.

"For the first 10 years of the Dapper Dan, the majority of the Pennsylvania squad was from the western half of the

5

state," he said, "and it kicked butt. I defy anyone to find any region at any time that had more talent than Pittsburgh did back then.

"Look at the trajectory of the power conferences [in college], specifically the ACC, and even the teams that later formed the Big East. All of them had players from our area."

Westinghouse's Maurice Stokes, Farrell's Julius McCoy, Willie Somerset, and Jack Marin, Wampum's Don Hennon, Midland's Norm Van Lier, and Ambridge's Dick DeVenzio and Dennis Wuycik were some of the forerunners responsible for the reputation that Western Pennsylvania slowly gained as a hotbed for recruiters. Except for Stokes, the 1956 NBA Rookie of the Year whose life was tragically cut short by a devastating basketball injury, all propelled their high schools to state championships.

McCoy's 27.2 points and 10 rebounds per game as a senior at Michigan State in 1955-56 earned him All-American status. After a stellar career at Duquesne, Somerset was an ABA All-Star in 1969. Marin competed in two Final Fours at Duke and was an NBA All-Star for the Bullets in 1972 and the Rockets in 1973. Hennon excelled at Pitt and in 1957-58 was selected to the same All-American team as Chamberlain, Elgin Baylor, Oscar Robertson, and Guy Rodgers. Van Lier went to St. Francis (Pa.) and enjoyed a decade-long NBA career, leading the league in assists in 1970-71 with the Cincinnati Royals. He later played in three All-Star games with the Bulls. DeVenzio—about whom Vaccaro said "there aren't enough superlatives to describe him"—was a first-team scholastic All-American in 1967 ahead of Spencer Haywood, Artis Gilmore, and Austin Carr. He then led Duke in assists three seasons in a row. Wuycik attended North Carolina and suited up in the ABA for Carolina Cougars coach Larry Brown.

With the 'Burgh supporting ballers of that caliber, the business-minded Vaccaro, a newly minted graduate of Youngstown State in the early '60s, heard opportunity knocking. He pounced on the chance to, as he said, "flaunt the state's talent," and it launched a career that forever changed the way athletes are promoted.

By the birth of the 1970s, Braddock's Billy Knight, Gus Gerard of Laurel Highlands, and Peabody's Melvin Bennett were carrying the torch for Pittsburgh-area hoops. In successive seasons with the Pacers, Knight finished second behind Julius Erving, then Pete Maravich for ABA and NBA scoring titles. During Gerard's junior year at Virginia, only N.C. State's David Thompson scored at a higher rate in the ACC. Gerard then started in the frontcourt for the Spirits of St. Louis, alongside Marvin Barnes. And the 6-8 Bennett turned pro after averaging a double-double as a freshman at Pitt, posting 12.1 points and 7.0 rebounds per game as a 21-year-old rookie for the Virginia Squires.

Indeed, Western Pennsylvania, known mostly to the sports world for its gridiron greats, has proven over time it has more to offer than just a preposterous number of quarterbacks known simply by their surnames: Unitas, Namath, Montana, Marino, and Kelly.

While this region has supplied the next levels of basketball with myriad talent, no one school in Western Pennsylvania—and few in the state—has come close to matching Schenley's tradition of excellence on the hardwood.

III. The Hill District

SCHENLEY DREW A LARGE PERCENTAGE of its students—and nearly every one of its basketball players—from the Hill District, the hub of African-American life in Pittsburgh. The Hill fell on hard times during the last half of the 20th century, but its storied and vibrant past can't be denied. It gained its nickname, Little Harlem, in the 1930s, as the Crawford Grill, one of the hottest jazz clubs in America, attracted some of the biggest acts in music. Gus Greenlee, its owner, used funds from his business of bootlegging and racketeering to open The Grill. He also bought a baseball team to compete in the Negro Leagues, and named it the Pittsburgh Crawfords. In 1932, he built Greenlee Field, the first black-owned park in the nation, and had the likes of Josh Gibson, Satchel Paige, and Cool Papa Bell on his payroll during the Great Depression.

The Pythian Temple, located between Wylie and Centre avenues, was another venue where blacks soaked up the riffs and runs of artists like Duke Ellington, Louis Armstrong, and Ella Fitzgerald. The Black Knights of Pythias, the local chapter of a fraternal organization of African-American construction workers, built the temple in 1928 to serve as its social center.

"When I was a young man, living in The Hill was like being in Times Square," 89-year-old Thomas Burks told the *Pittsburgh Tribune-Review* in 2014. "The whole area was lit up all night long."

Headquartered in The Hill, the *Pittsburgh Courier* became one of the nation's most renowned black newspapers. It worked as an instrument for social progress, and its circulation reached 400,000 with 14 regional editions.

The Hill was a city within the city, but its downward spiral began in the late 1950s when the government displaced approximately 8,000 residents and 400 businesses to construct the Civic Arena. The Crawford Grill was demolished to pave way for what became home to the Pittsburgh Penguins. Federally-funded public housing was then introduced to the neighborhood in massive numbers, and many middle-class families fled.

> The Hill District fell on hard times during the last half of the 20th century, but its storied and vibrant past can't be denied.

The assassination of Martin Luther King, Jr. in April 1968 incited riots that set The Hill ablaze. Almost 500 fires culminated in 926 arrests and more than $500,000 of property damage. Several people suffered gunshot wounds. The insurrection was preceded by a lack of equal opportunities for blacks, particularly in Pittsburgh's labor and trade unions, and the general unrest stemming from the Vietnam War.

"I was shocked, and I was hurt," said Dennis Biggs, a retired a Pittsburgh police officer who was a 17-year-old student at Schenley when King died. "It was evil striking down a person who was trying to do good in the world.

"But I couldn't understand why all the looting and burning was going on, especially in areas where primarily black people lived. We were destroying where we lived."

John Edwin Hicks, a retired draftsman, was serving in Vietnam back then, and he believes that the damage done to businesses more than 40 years ago has discouraged other merchants from moving into The Hill.

"I just don't think people consider this a viable business area after all the burning and rioting and looting," Hicks said. "They just didn't want to come back."

Robert Johnson was a 31-year-old postal worker who said nothing positive came out of the riots.

"Younger people didn't pay too much attention [to the consequences]," Johnson said. "Older people realized it didn't help out nothing. It didn't save nothing. They just destroyed [things] for themselves."

Three thousand National Guardsmen descended upon The Hill, adding to the 1,000 city and state police officers already stationed there, and enforced a curfew from 7 p.m. to 5 a.m. City Safety Director David Craig told the media that the violence followed a "pattern of individually inclined hoodlums."

The Associated Press issued commentary from ground zero in The Hill.

"Gangs of vandals pitched firebombs and stormed liquor stores, and a lumber yard burned down," it reported. "Police investigated dozens of complaints from jittery residents worried about prowlers, suspicious cars, and even the possibility the drinking water reservoir had been poisoned."

Twenty-four hours later, the tattered streets were virtually abandoned.

"The streets along The Hill, where 50,000 Negroes live in a ghetto that covers not much more than a square mile, were almost deserted, except for the troops," the *Press* said. "Six to a dozen guardsmen or state police stood at every intersection with bayonets at the ready. Crowds that had taunted and peppered them with rocks melted away. Some residents even brought coffee to the men standing guard."

Less than a year before the riots, Bob Pease, who was the executive director of the Pittsburgh Urban Redevelopment Authority back then, spoke of the conditions that precipitated the mayhem.

"There's one thing I found out after spending so much time in The Hill," Pease said in 1967. "Pittsburgh's three biggest problems are education, employment, and housing—in that order. We forget sometimes that people are poor for only one reason: They don't have any money. A job is the product of an education. A house is the product of a job."

As the 20th century came to a close, the plunge into crime and decadence only continued. Michael Fuoco of the *Pittsburgh Post-Gazette* examined the Hill District's "lost greatness" in a series of articles in 1999.

"Near the corner of Centre Avenue and Kirkpatrick Street," Fuoco wrote, "40 men are hanging out, waiting for the dope man. Down the street, a building is under consideration as the site of a planned liaison center where addicts, the unemployed, and the homeless can connect easily with the agencies they need. In a dilapidated house not far away, a young, single mother struggles to find enough food to feed her hungry children."

Now, almost half of The Hill's population lives below the poverty level. According to police figures, The Hill contains one apartment complex alone that in 2008 averaged five murders for every 100 households.

The Rev. Glenn Grayson of Wesley Center A.M.E. Zion Church on Herron Avenue in The Hill had a long time before grown weary of doing funerals for young victims of gun violence. For a number of years, his eulogies were always for someone else's child.

Until October 2010, when it was for his own.

His son, Jeron Grayson, a recent Schenley graduate and freshman studying business at Hampton University, was an innocent bystander when he was slain at a party on his first visit home from college. (A 19-year-old man from Monessen was denied entry to the off-campus party at California University of Pennsylvania. He later returned to the scene with a gun, firing at the group of revelers. Grayson, at the wrong place at the wrong time, was hit in the torso by one of the slugs and was pronounced dead a few hours later.)

"As a pastor and an advocate of anti-violence, in my wildest dreams, I never thought I'd be doing my own child's funeral," said Rev. Grayson. "My son had so much potential and so many dreams. Two families are shattered now, because both lost a son. Black families are being shattered every day, and I don't know what the answer is. But we need to come up with one, because no one should have to bury their child."

Jeron was an All-City League defensive back and running back for the Spartans, and as a senior, he helped them win their first City League football title in a decade.

"I really love my kids," Schenley coach Jason Bell said after his team's double-overtime defeat of Oliver in the 2009 championship game. "Kids on this team have lost parents this season. This won't hit them until later on when they're older. They'll come back to their 50th high school reunion and talk about this game."

Bell, of course, had no way of knowing that Grayson, who scored on a 29-yard rush in the second quarter of that game, would be dead in less than a year.

"It's so important that we honor the legacy of Dr. King, and continue to strive toward his vision," said Rev. Grayson. "Almost 50 years later, you would think that his speeches would be somewhat antiquated. Unfortunately, I believe they're still very relevant, and today's youth face a lot of the same challenges as previous generations."

The eyesores of boarded-up storefronts, decrepit row homes, and potholed streets unmistakably project a melancholy not likely to draw tourists to the The Hill any time soon. While visitors to Pittsburgh continue to invade PNC Park, walk the Allegheny Riverfront, scale Mount Washington, and inhale sandwiches from Primanti Brothers, they won't find advertisements for The Hill in any of their travel guides. And companies like Starbucks have no plans to add to their portfolio by plowing any of the rubble-strewn lots where grass grows through the cracks in the concrete.

IV. Schenley's Finest

ERECTED IN **1916,** Schenley High School, located at the edge of The Hill in Pittsburgh's North Oakland neighborhood, was the first high school in the United States that cost a million dollars to build. The expansive, triangular-shaped structure is a city landmark, having dominated the intersection of Bigelow Boulevard and Centre Avenue for almost a century, and is listed on the National Register of Historic Places.

With a façade of Indiana limestone, the school was named after Mary Schenley, one of Pittsburgh's most prominent philanthropists of the 19th century. (Much in the city still bears her name: a tunnel, bridge, hotel, plaza, and park.) In the arenas of arts, academia, and athletics, the school has produced an array of winners. Andy Warhol was the pioneer of pop art whose *Campbell's Soup Cans* are recognized in every nook and cranny of the world, and his paintings are among some of the most expensive ever sold. Jazz musician George Benson has 10 Grammy Awards and a triple-platinum album to his credit. Physicist Cliff Shull earned a Nobel Prize for his contributions to the study of condensed matter. Bruno Sammartino's reign as champion of the World Wrestling Federation lasted longer than Hulk Hogan's. Running back Larry Brown found the end zone 12 times in 12 games for the Washington Redskins in 1972 and was thus crowned the NFL's MVP.

This distinguished list doesn't even mention any of the basketball-playing alumni who enhanced the spotlight on Western Pennsylvania hoops and kept them on the map for years to come.

The Class of 1967's Kenny Durrett and Ed "Petie" Gibson powered the Spartans to their first PIAA title as juniors. Durrett, a *Parade* magazine All-American, was a 6-8 forward ahead of his time in terms of his ability to face the basket, knock down the 15-footer, or attack the rim with athleticism unusual for his size. As a senior at La Salle, the adopted folk hero of Philadelphia averaged 27.0 points and 9.3 boards before shredding his knee late in the season and never being the same again. Durrett was still the fourth overall pick of that spring's NBA draft, a testament to how skilled he was.

The 5-7 Gibson—the grandson of Josh Gibson, the "Black Babe Ruth"—started three years at New Mexico. In Albuquerque, the petite playmaker ran legendary coach Bob King's offense, doing his part to fill The Pit during its infancy by dishing out more than seven assists per game.

Courtesy of the University of New Mexico
Ed "Petie" Gibson remains one of New Mexico's all-time leaders in assists.

Maurice Lucas and Ricky Coleman, both of the Class of 1971, and Robert "Jeep" Kelley, Class of 1973, lifted Schenley to its second crown when the former two were seniors. Their coach, Spencer Watkins, deemed the court a canvas, allowing their talents to flourish free from the restriction of a structured offense.

"I look at basketball as an art form," Watkins said before the Spartans painted a Rembrandt in their 77-60 victory over Norristown in the final. "Each player is an artist who is given a pattern to work in. But then he has to come up with his own thing. I try to put myself in their shoes. If you take a kid out of the ghetto, then try to change his lifestyle, you've really lost the ball game even if you win."

Lucas, a 6-9 banger and late bloomer, starred at Marquette under coach Al McGuire and won an NBA ring with the Portland Trail Blazers. The four-time All-Star was a rugged enforcer known best for squaring off with Gilmore and Darryl Dawkins.

Courtesy of Marquette University

As a junior at Marquette in 1973-74, Maurice Lucas averaged a double-double, helping the Warriors advance to the national championship game before turning pro.

"When you take high school, college, and the pros into consideration," Vaccaro said, "Maurice was the best player to ever come out of Pittsburgh."

As a 6-3 slasher, Coleman's 21.2 points and 4.6 assists per outing at Jacksonville University in 1974-75 prompted the Boston Celtics to draft him in the sixth round. And Kelley's career as a floor general had the potential to go the distance. However, he dropped out of UNLV two months into his freshman year and was ruled ineligible at Hawaii, before drifting into drugs.

During his junior year, Nathan "Sonny" Lewis, Class of 1976, and his teammates secured the program's third championship. The 6-3 jumping jack with a 46-inch vertical leap played two seasons at Pitt before clashing with the coach and finishing his career as an NAIA All-American at Point Park College in downtown Pittsburgh. He and Kelley were half-brothers.

*Courtesy of
Jacksonville University*
Ricky Coleman (21 points) was one of five Spartans to score in double figures in Schenley's 77-60 win over Norristown in the 1971 PIAA final.

Calvin Kane, Class of 1978, and Larry Anderson, Class of 1979, enabled the Spartans to collect their fourth PIAA trophy when Schenley toppled Lebanon and its giant junior, Sam Bowie, by one point in the '78 final. If not for their clutch performances 10 days earlier in the first round of the playoffs, the Spartans would have been spectators and not contestants in the championship game. Kane scored eight of his 13 points in the third quarter and Anderson struck for 25 points, including Schenley's last 10, in a 62-61 victory over Wilkinsburg. The pair negated the 20 points and 20 rebounds furnished by Wilkinsburg's Bruce Atkins, a 6-7 forward bound for Duquesne and a fourth-round pick of the 76ers in 1982.

The Spartans were lathered up to face the 7-0 Bowie, who was becoming the subject of one of the most intense recruiting wars that college coaches had ever waged.

"If Sam were a high school kid [during the days when they could skip college to enter the pros], no one would recruit him, because he would be the No. 1 pick in the NBA draft," said former UNLV coach Jerry Tarkanian. "He was that good. Back then, every school in the country coveted him." (Bowie eventually signed with Kentucky, which, according to Tarkanian, gave him a Cadillac and a hotel room in Central Pennsylvania to use whenever he wished. Bowie's legacy is one of injuries and unfulfilled expectations. And he'll always be known as the man the Trail Blazers drafted ahead of Michael Jordan, not to mention John Stockton and Charles Barkley.)

Courtesy of UNLV
Larry Anderson was a third-round draft pick of the Cleveland Cavaliers.

Wherever Lebanon had played that season and the next, tickets were nearly impossible to come by, as Bowie's reputation had certainly preceded him.

One newspaper columnist likened the action that evening at Hersheypark Arena, the site where Wilt Chamberlain once scored 100 points in an NBA game, to combat. He even drew upon religious history to express the fervor before tip-off.

"There was no diplomatic break of relations, nor any hastily called congressional vote to declare war," wrote Terry Bowser of the *Huntingdon Daily News*. "Nonetheless, it was 'war' when battle-hardened Pittsburgh Schenley fought raw-recruit Lebanon for the basketball throne. The trenches were dug well before the opening salvo. Ticket-scalpers were busy trying to peddle their wares outside the main entrance to the 7,200-seat arena as empty-handed late-comers pondered the asking price. Wide lines of fans a couple hundred yards long snaked their way through the parking lot over an hour before game time. To the disgruntlement of advance ticket buyers, there were no reserved seats, and eager fans were primed for the mad scramble once the gates finally opened. There wasn't a vacant seat in the house when a couple hundred reinforcements from Schenley flowed into the aisles and stairways at the 11th hour. The PIAA set up temporary seating on the arena floor behind the Spartan bench for their followers. It resembled what must have taken place at Rome's Coliseum as the pious Romans cried for the lions to be loosed on the humble Christians."

Following the 51-50 victory, during which the Cedars turned the ball over 19 times, "the psyched-up Spartans, obviously enjoying their spoils of war, were roaming the confines of the arena floor in full uniform a half-hour after the battle smoke had cleared."

On the next level, Kane was a point guard at Lamar University under coach Billy Tubbs when the Cardinals surprisingly reached the Sweet 16 in 1980. At UNLV, the 6-7 Anderson christened the newly opened Thomas & Mack Center and formed a destructive one-two punch with Sidney Green when the Rebels sat atop the polls in 1983.

Mark Halsel, Class of 1980, signed a letter of intent with Robert Morris, but had a change of heart and accepted a scholarship from Northeastern and coach Jim Calhoun.

(The letter wasn't binding because Northeastern was one of the few colleges that did not subscribe to it.) Four years later, the 6-6 Halsel played every position except point guard, escorted the Huskies to a pair of NCAA Tournament appearances, became the ECAC North (now the America East Conference) Player of the Year, and finished as the program's all-time leading rebounder.

"You don't grow up in Pittsburgh and play ball without knowing how to rebound," Halsel said. "I played basketball in a lot of places, but Pittsburgh was the toughest because of the people. Everybody there works hard at what they do, and the same is true of basketball. Kids there work to get the ball."

Halsel once snared 18 boards in a game against Georgia's Dominique Wilkins and ultimately earned an invite from Bobby Knight to the 1984 Olympic Trials. There, Michael Jordan and Chris Mullin edged out Halsel for roster spots at swingman.

"Mark believed every rebound would be his," said Calhoun, the New England lifer who later won three national championships at Connecticut. "He never stopped going after the ball and wearing opponents out. Defensively, we had him guard 6-11 centers and 6-1 guards, and he did a good job on them all."

There were other Schenley greats who earned Division I scholarships for the skills they honed as adolescents in The Hill, but these men were the best of the bunch. Unfortunately, though, most of them now have one thing in common with their alma mater.

V. Schenley's Makeover

SCHENLEY QUICKLY REACHED the peak of its enrollment in 1940 with 3,012 students. By 1983, however, it had all the trappings of an inner-city school: a mounting dropout rate, woeful academic performance, a nearly all-black student body, and pride in little else other than athletics. Whites comprised only 14 percent of the school's population, since most of the area's white families escaped by finding a way for their children to attend Taylor Allderdice High School in the nearby Squirrel Hill section of the city.

Schenley, simply put, was in need of a transformation. John Young became principal of his alma mater in 1980, and he had his work cut out for him.

"Many students sat out in front of the building—sometimes all day long," Young told the *Post-Gazette* in 1988. "Their behavior certainly wasn't good. We got many complaints from the residents."

Back then, a food truck peddling candy and snacks had parked across the street from the school and tempted students to cut class. A city ordinance restricted the truck from parking less than 500 feet from the school, and Young measured the distance, confirming that it was too close.

"The man who operated the truck told me I was threatening his livelihood," he said.

Young enacted a rule that would suspend for three days any kid caught on the other side of Bigelow Boulevard. It worked.

"We had to break a lot of bad habits, even in the building," Young said. "Students were not in the habit of going to school on time. It took a long time to convince them that we were serious."

With students back in the classroom where they belonged, the administration aimed to keep them there by doing more to stoke their interest in learning. Young instituted awards assemblies to boost morale and school spirit. Suddenly, it was cool to be smart at Schenley.

In order to attain more racial balance at Schenley, the Pittsburgh Public Schools then inaugurated a magnet program centered on international studies and technology. The new curriculum was designed to draw more high-achieving students. Also, the school was renamed the Schenley High School Teacher Center. It was a grand experiment that cost taxpayers more than a million dollars per year, but the move resuscitated the school.

> By 1983, Schenley had all the trappings of an inner-city school: a mounting dropout rate, woeful academic performance, and a nearly all-black student body.

Seventy-five of Pittsburgh's best secondary teachers were chosen from a pool of 180 applicants to run the new incarnation of Schenley. At one point from 1983-1987, every other teacher in the district left their school, having been replaced by a trained substitute, and cycled through Schenley in groups of 48 for an eight-week training period.

It functioned as a mini-sabbatical, during which the more than 900 high school teachers in the city refined their skills and participated in seminars. The idea behind The Teacher Center was that many instructors can get stale midway through their careers, and that teachers could do a better job than anyone else of helping one another.

"For years, secondary teachers have gone into their classes, and no one has bothered to look at what they do," said Judy Johnston, the Center's director. "The thinking was that the teachers somehow were just going to be in there and do what needed to be done. This has given them time to reflect on their teaching. It's rejuvenated them."

"The Schenley High School Teacher Center is the most exciting development in in-service teacher education in America," said Lee Shulman, then the president of the American Educational Research Association.

The unique program garnered national headlines and fulfilled its goal of increasing student proficiency throughout all of the city's secondary schools. In 1987, Schenley was picked as one of three Western Pennsylvania schools of excellence by the U.S. Department of Education.

"It's amazing the feedback I would get when I went to an education conference in another city," Young said. "As soon as someone found out I was from Schenley, the focus of the meeting changed. Sometimes, the rest of the meeting was spent picking my brain about what's going on here."

In 1989, Young called upon the non-profit Pittsburgh Mediation Center to initiate a program that would enable Schenley students to settle their differences with their mouths instead of their fists.

"We found that in many of the student disputes, if we could just get the students together, they basically solved the problems themselves," he said. "They needed to learn that responsibility."

The students who completed the mediator training were awarded diplomas by a judge in a courtroom ceremony, during which they took oaths swearing to be fair and impartial and to maintain confidentiality.

The renaissance at Schenley was undoubtedly afoot.

VI. Climbing the Hill

FRED SKROCKI WAS RAISED in a blue-collar family on the North Side of Pittsburgh and earned his bachelor's degree from Slippery Rock University. He was 32 years old, teaching health and physical education at Herron Hill Junior High, when he was tapped as one of the 75 teachers that would manage the new Schenley.

With a passion for basketball, a solid resume in education, but virtually no coaching experience, Skrocki was hoping to catch on as an assistant with Schenley in 1983. Instead, he was granted the head post.

"All of the Schenley coaching jobs were up for grabs because they were starting over with a whole new faculty," Skrocki said. "I always loved basketball, but I never played it a very high level. I was definitely surprised to be named the head coach, and there may have been some resentment from people in the community.

"I understood very quickly the pressure associated with the position. Like if we didn't win, it was my fault. I remember coming off the court one game and a little girl— she couldn't have been more than eight—told me that I sucked."

Throughout the 1980s and 1990s, Pittsburgh was no longer a petri dish of prime talent, much to Skrocki's chagrin. Eighteen years into his tenure at Schenley, Eastern Pennsylvania schools, powered by their NBA-stars-in-the-making, had established their authority in the PIAA's largest classification (4A). Billy Owens carried Carlisle to four consecutive titles. Lower Merion's Kobe Bryant, Plymouth-Whitemarsh's John Salmons, and Chester's Jameer Nelson all guided their squads to championships.

Darrick Suber (Class of 1989) and Jeff Benson (1995) were arguably the cream of the crop that Skrocki coached during that period, but none of them could lead the Spartans to even a Pittsburgh City League title.

Suber, a 6-3 guard, averaged 28.3 points per game as a senior at Schenley. His 2,219 points at Rider College are still the most in school history, and his heroics as a senior in 1993 are relived annually during college basketball's championship week. Down a point to Wagner with four seconds left in the Northeast Conference title tilt, the host Broncs had possession of the ball 94 feet from their basket. Suber cradled the in-bounds pass in front of Wagner's bench, traversed the floor in four dribbles, and drilled a floater from the elbow at the buzzer. The Shot, as it has since become known on campus, punched

Courtesy of
Rider University
Darrick Suber, shown here with Rider coach Kevin Bannon, is the Broncs' all-time leading scorer. His buzzer-beater in the 1993 Northeast Conference championship game is the stuff of legends.

26

Rider's ticket to the Big Dance and unleashed a flood of ecstasy throughout the 2,000 fans in attendance and millions more watching on ESPN.

"I was supposed to be a decoy on the play," Suber said. "And if you're from The Hill and played at Schenley, the idea of being a decoy doesn't sit well with you. One thing I'd learned about the end of close games was that the other team would be nervous and not want to foul. Sure enough, my defender backed off, so I got the ball and went straight down the court. And when I let it go, I knew it was good."

Never mind that, a week later, the Broncs trailed Jamal Mashburn-led Kentucky by 39 points at halftime and lost by 44 in the first round of the NCAA Tournament. Suber's shot is a microcosm of the magic that is March Madness, and in the Information Age of Internet searches and YouTube videos, it will be replayed in perpetuity.

Benson, competing for the Community College of Beaver County in 1997, scored to break a tie with one second left in the junior-college championship game and give the Titans a national title. The shooting guard then transferred to Division II Bloomsburg University, where he was the Pennsylvania State Athletic Conference East Division Player of the Year as a senior in 1999.

Despite all the feathers Suber and Benson put in their caps on the next level, their teams at Schenley lacked depth, and they could never get the Spartans over the hump.

The new millennium, however, finally brought Skrocki a roster that could contend for PIAA laurels. In 2000-01, it featured three Division I prospects: Nate Gerwig (Kent State), Jack Higgins (Cleveland State/Duquesne), and Shawn Hawkins (Long Beach State). Schenley advanced to the final in Hershey, but fell 70-57 to Coatesville and Seton Hall-bound forward John Allen, *The Associated Press* Player of the Year. The score wasn't indicative of how close the

Courtesy of
Kent State University
Nate Gerwig cracked the starting lineup at Kent State as a freshman in 2001-2002, when the Golden Flashes won the Mid-American Conference and advanced to the Elite Eight.

contest was, as there were 13 lead changes in the first three quarters, and the Spartans trailed by one point with three minutes left.

The outcome could have been accounted for in the disparity of free throws each team shot. The Red Raiders went to the line 29 times, connecting on 26, while the Spartans, feeling like the victims of a heist, never made it there. The game is a pill that remains hard for Skrocki to swallow.

"Nate had a welt on the side of his head and a cut under his eye, but we didn't get any calls," he said. "I always tried to teach the part off the court, too. Somewhere along the line, maybe that experience was going to help them. Maybe they'd realize that sometimes you work your butt off, but you just don't get what you want."

The 6-8 Gerwig would soon start as a freshman for the Golden Flashes when their Cinderella run in the 2002 NCAA Tournament ended in the Elite Eight. He'd even punctuate his pro career, spent mostly in Europe, by playing in the NBA Development League with the Fort Wayne (Ind.) Mad Ants. But he could never cleanse his palate of the bitter aftertaste of falling to Coatesville.

"Never in my life have I heard of a team not going to the foul line at least once," said Gerwig. "It's a shame it had to happen in a game of that magnitude. When we looked at the stats, it took some of the hurt of losing away, because there was nothing we could've done. We were playing five against eight."

Five years later, on the last day of the 2005-06 season, Schenley returned to Chocolate Town as the favorites against Lower Merion.

VII. The Anatomy of a Contender

WITH ONLY ONE SENIOR in their rotation, the Spartans had a foundation of youth that had originally been laid when the boys were seven and eight years old and first getting to know one another in The Hill.

At 6-6 and almost 250 pounds as a junior, DeJuan Blair was the fulcrum of an offense that punished on the inside and ran with the horsepower of a stock car on the outside. Regardless of whether it was in high school, college, or the pros, Blair has always played bigger than his height would allow, courtesy of broad shoulders, a seven-foot wingspan, and outlandish strength that opens up paths to the bucket.

Blair's current prowess on the highest level of basketball is remarkable, considering how he tore the ACL in each of his knees as a freshman and sophomore at Schenley and was sidelined for 16 months.

"I can still see DeJuan as a ninth-grader, hopping around the gym on one foot, trying to show everyone that he could still dunk," Skrocki said. "His knee eventually healed, but the next year [in the state quarterfinals], he hurt the other one. For him to come back the way he did as a junior, it was just incredible."

DeJuan and his other siblings gather their inspiration from DeMond, their brother who died when he rolled off the bed at three months old. And they got their game from their parents, Greg and Shari Blair. Greg, a teammate of Darrick

Courtesy of Eric Hartline
DeJuan Blair muscles away a rebound from an opponent.

Suber, graduated from Schenley in 1991 and played for Skrocki, while the former Shari Saddler averaged 20 points and 20 rebounds a contest at Serra Catholic in nearby McKeesport.

"I was never a troublemaker, but I don't know where my life would be without basketball," he said. "I'm glad my mom and dad put one in my hands."

As a youngster, DeJuan was a fixture at the Ammon Recreation Center and at Kennard Park in The Hill, just like his future Schenley teammates were. It's where they cut their teeth and inherited the swagger of their predecessors who never gave them any credit and swore they would never be as good.

As a 6-5 junior, D.J. Kennedy was a crafty southpaw, as resourceful as MacGyver, and a triple-double threat in every game he played. His father, David Kennedy Sr., won a PIAA title alongside NFL lineman Sam Clancy at Fifth Avenue High School, which shuttered in 1976.

(To address concerns about de facto segregation in the 1970s, Fifth Avenue and Gladstone merged to form Brashear High School, which welcomed more than 5,000 students to its new building on Crane Avenue in Beechview. Fifth Avenue had educated students in the Lower Hill, while Schenley's territory included the Middle and Upper Hill. Kennedy and Clancy's Archers earned a national ranking as high as No. 2, despite the uncertainty surrounding their 1975-76 season. The strike by the Pittsburgh Federation of Teachers spanned 56 calendar days and 33 school days in December and January, and jeopardized Fifth Avenue's last crusade before it even began. It eventually got under way, and the Archers, a nickname inspired by their school's Gothic-style architecture, won all 15 of their games on the path to the crown. "The strike was really a drag," said Clancy, Pitt's all-time leading rebounder. "We knew we were good but never had the chance to prove it. Maybe that's why the [PIAA] tournament meant so much to us. We were glad to see the strike end, but I'm not sure the rest of the state was.")

An accomplished quarterback, the elder Kennedy concentrated on hoops in college at Cincinnati, and the Dallas Mavericks took a flier on him in the eighth round of the 1981 draft, although he never made the league.

"I had a lot of motivation early on to live up to my father's name," said D.J., who lived with his mother growing up. "I was always hearing from older dudes about how great of an athlete he was, but he didn't push me. He gave me space to choose my own way.

"I looked up more to my brother [Derrick Holliday]. He was four years older than me, and didn't make the best decisions with his life. He's always had good intentions, but he got caught up in a lot of bad situations. Regardless, he always shielded me from the streets and did whatever he could to keep me on the right track."

Courtesy of Eric Hartline
D.J. Kennedy attacks the basket.

Jamaal Bryant, nicknamed "Onion" since he was a tyke when one of his youth coaches said his head looked like a bulb, stood just 5-9 and weighed 140 pounds as a junior. An artist at the point, he used the floor as his canvas and mesmerized crowds with fancy ballhandling and no-look passing. The mercurial playmaker saw the floor as clearly as anyone in Western Pennsylvania back then and could toss alley-oops to Blair and Kennedy in his sleep.

"My role?" Bryant asked. "To do whatever it took to win. I had to win, needed to win. I couldn't stand losing. It was like coming face to face with death. I used to cry for hours after a loss."

As a sophomore at Schenley, DeAndre Kane tried to use every minute of the 2005-06 season to make up for lost time. Kane didn't play as a freshman, because he refused to carry the upperclassmen's bags, perhaps foreshadowing some of the troubles he'd have later on in his career.

"DeAndre had the mentality that he didn't have to listen," said Bryant. "He was definitely uncoachable at first."

The enigmatic Kane blossomed into a 6-4 point guard at the next level. But as a 10th-grader, he was a few inches shorter, playing off the ball, and carving out his niche on the team, all while trying to not get swallowed up by the streets.

Like Kennedy, Kane had championship blood coursing through his veins, as his father Calvin had steered the Spartans to their last state crown 28 long winters ago.

"Life was difficult in The Hill," Kane said. "Everywhere you looked, there were cautionary tales, examples of someone who could've been the one to make it big, but the streets took over. It would've been easy for me or any of my Schenley teammates to get stuck in that life and end up dead or in jail like so many others.

"Growing up, we were stupid, young and stupid. We'd go to parties wearing red bandanas, thinking we were gangbangers. With all the stuff I saw and what people were into, I'm fortunate to still be here."

Kane had a girlfriend and another friend who were murdered in separate incidents during his youth. The former was killed in a drive-by shooting, and Kane made it to the scene in time to see paramedics covering up her body. The latter died when he and Kane were at a party,

DeAndre Kane found his stride as a sophomore, and wanted nothing more than to be like his father Calvin, who won a state title at Schenley.

and tempers began to flare. They left the house just before shots rang out, and were running toward their car when Kane's friend caught a bullet in the head.

Kane was and remains best friends with the last piece to Schenley's puzzle.

At 6-2, Greg Blair Jr., another sophomore, never sprouted like DeJuan, but his appetite for physicality may have exceeded his brother's.

"I was the guy who gave us the spark," Greg said. "When we needed a hard foul, I was the one to do it. And I loved that role.

"I always played basketball in DeJuan's shadow, but having him there was a blessing, because it took the pressure off me."

Schenley's offense fired on all cylinders when DeJuan was drop-stepping through traffic, Kennedy was gliding to the rim from seemingly impossible angles, Onion was slicing up his defenders with his crossover, Kane was bombing from distance, and Greg was whooping it up and bullying the opposition.

VIII. Coming up Short

In 2005-06, Lower Merion boasted a pair of all-state seniors—Ryan Brooks (Temple) and Garrett Williamson (Saint Joseph's)—who would fashion decent college careers in the Big 5. And they were up for the challenges looming in March.

To merit their date with Schenley, the Aces, three days prior at the Palestra, had to outscore Chester, 33-18, in the fourth quarter. They had scrapped together a run in one of the most hallowed basketball buildings in the country, and the sequence became as much a part of their lore as Kobe's fabled career. Lower Merion had outlasted the same team that beat it not only in the District One final but in the previous year's PIAA final.

"We were riding high after that win," said Brooks, now a pro in Germany. "We got our revenge against Chester, and were clearly the underdogs against Schenley. We knew that we had to put together a complete game in order to win. For one more night, we needed to buckle down, defend well, and make the right decisions."

Schenley swiftly validated the reason most sportswriters picked it to win by racing out to a 9-0 lead before its opponent could breathe.

"Everyone in the state was saying Schenley was this big, bad wolf from Pittsburgh," said Lower Merion coach Gregg Downer. "If we played them 10 times, we probably would've only won twice. They had that much talent and athleticism.

But to be honest, I saw glaring weaknesses with some of the stuff they ran, and we thought we could expose them."

Downer called a timeout midway through the first quarter and implemented a triangle-and-two defense, and his troops responded with an 18-4 run. "It was like a game of cat and mouse," he said, "the way we switched up our strategy to try to keep them guessing."

Despite Schenley's four-point lead at the break, Kennedy was so frustrated by all of the turnovers the Spartans had committed that he initially refused to come out after intermission.

"D.J. knocked the clipboard out of the hands of one of the assistant coaches," Kane said, adding that none of the X's and O's drawn up that night worked. "So he had to sit the first few minutes of the half."

"I had a bad feeling about what was going to happen in the second half," Kennedy said. "It was a

> "It was like getting knocked out in the last second of a title fight. I'd have rather lost by 40."
>
> **—DeJuan Blair**

weird game. Just different. They came with a plan and executed it to perfection. The game meant so much to us, to our community, but they out-smarted us and left us in tears."

His premonition was accurate, and the finish had more suspense than a Hitchcock film.

With Schenley trailing by a point with less a minute remaining, Blair missed a runner and Kane bricked up a pull-up jumper. And in the waning seconds, Kennedy was blocked twice during a scramble underneath the basket.

The Aces prevailed, 60-58.

"It was like getting knocked out in the last second of a title fight," DeJuan Blair said. "I'd have rather lost by 40."

"I didn't go to school for like three weeks after that game," Bryant said. "I'm not kidding. I was so sick of people saying that I should keep my head up because we were so close, and that was an accomplishment."

So demoralized were the Spartans in the aftermath of the loss that Skrocki had to pick up three silver medals that were left behind in the locker room of the Giant Center.

Thus began the narrative of the 2006-07 edition of the Schenley Spartans, one of the best outfits in the annals of Western Pennsylvania basketball.

IX. Making History

THE PAIN OF THE LOSS to Lower Merion eventually subsided, and when it did, Schenley's nucleus regrouped, setting the school's state-title drought of almost three decades in its crosshairs. Kennedy, however, was still reeling, although this time it had nothing to do with basketball.

In the summer of 2006, his brother, Derrick Holliday, almost died in his arms after being shot seven times in the lower body. (In a 2009 story about Kennedy, the *New York Post* incorrectly reported that the shooting occurred a year later, in 2007.)

"When I got to the scene, I remember Derrick lying on the ground, looking into my eyes," Kennedy said. "He kept saying that he was going to make it, and I kept telling him, 'You can't go out like this.'"

It took two surgeries for Holliday to survive the shooting, but the ordeal understandably shook Kennedy to the core.

"I was thinking of transferring out of the city for my senior year," he said. "Psychologically, there was a lot of stuff weighing on me with my brother and all. The Hill isn't a very safe place; you always have to watch where you go. And I was leaning toward getting out."

"Not many people knew that D.J. was close to leaving," Skrocki said. "He had all the off-the-court distractions, and on the court, I think there were times when he didn't appreciate how we played from the inside-out."

Kennedy ultimately refused to abandon his friends and a shot at history.

"I couldn't leave that brotherhood," he said. "We were too close. We were confident that the state would be ours. We had a target on our back and a chip on our shoulder."

In a November interview with reporter Mike White of the *Post-Gazette*, Blair guaranteed that they'd be celebrating in March.

"Their mantra," Skrocki said, "was no egos, no excuses, no superstars. Just one goal: a state championship."

For added motivation, Skrocki often placed the neglected runner-up trophy on a stool at half court during practices. It was a reminder of the pain of coming up short and how the consolation prize—a memento that most other schools would cherish—was really no consolation at all.

"I was sick of looking at that thing," Kane said. "By the end of the season, nobody would even go within 10 feet of it. But it definitely made us work harder. We came out hungry."

The Spartans opened the campaign, during which they would travel thousands of miles, by dismembering a pair of City League rivals, Westinghouse by 46 points and Carrick by 60. They then trekked a half-hour up the Ohio River to Aliquippa, a once-thriving but now worn-out town beset by drugs and crime that harvested Mike Ditka, Tony Dorsett, Ty Law, and Darrelle Revis. The hosts had sold 3,000 tickets to the game, an astonishing amount considering it was only the second week of December.

"During warm-ups, both teams put on the most unbelievable display of dunking I've ever seen," White said. "The referees weren't there yet; they came late. I mean, even Onion was dunking. It was incredible. The crowd completely lost its mind."

An anticipated matchup in the post between Blair and his AAU comrade, 6-9 forward Herb Pope, never materialized, though, since Blair was plagued by foul trouble all evening. Pope, who would lead the Big East in rebounding at Seton Hall, rallied the Quips from a 16-point deficit, but the Spartans held on for a 68-65 win.

Ten days later, Schenley arrived in Fort Myers for the prestigious City of Palms Classic and justified the hype that accompanied them. They split four games against some of the top-flight teams in America. In an 88-75 setback against Florida's Lake Howell, they traded baskets with the Silver Hawks until Blair (29 points and 14 rebounds) picked up his fourth foul midway through the third quarter. The trio of Chandler Parsons, Nick Calathes, and Joey Rodriguez combined for 79 of Lake Howell's 88 points.

During its other loss in the Sunshine State, Schenley wasted 20 points from Kennedy and a 15-point lead before falling to Lance Stephenson's Lincoln Railsplitters.

Each team would win their respective state titles in Florida and New York.

"The group created an identity down there," Skrocki said. "We didn't even know if we'd be able to go, since each team was required to put up $1,500, with the rest covered by the tournament's sponsors. The school didn't have the money, but a generous alum stepped up and footed the whole bill. He knew it was the opportunity of a lifetime for a bunch of kids from the inner-city.

"So we went with the intention of having as much fun as we possibly could. Pizza parties by the pool, no curfews, and not much practice. The group really bonded. That is, until it was time to leave."

With the team on board its return flight, fatigued and waiting for take-off, Kane refused to turn off his cell phone. He stood his ground until the pilot dismissed the Spartans from the plane.

"Yeah, that was bad," Kane said. "I had never flown before, so I didn't think it was that big of a deal."

Said Bryant: "It didn't help that DeAndre was teasing one of the flight attendants because he was a guy. You can just imagine what he was saying."

"We're all tired and ready to fall asleep, and the next thing I know, DeAndre is getting into it with a flight attendant," Greg Blair said. "We had to wait three hours for another flight. This first one, we had all type of leg room. But the next one, we were so cramped and tight. I remember guys were pissed."

Kennedy was one of them.

"Looking back on it now, it was one of the funniest things I've ever seen," he said. "But I wasn't laughing then. I wanted to kill him."

In late January, Schenley grappled with Chester in a showcase event on the latter's turf, at Cardinal O'Hara High School in suburban Philadelphia. The Clippers represent Pennsylvania's gold standard in scholastic hoops, forged through eight PIAA championships in a 30-year span that commenced in 1983. Chester, situated on the Delaware River between Philadelphia and Wilmington, was once a city of economic promise but has been in decay since the 1960s when the shipping and auto plants began to fly the coop. Now, its poverty-stricken population lives and dies with the Clippers, and its streets are as violent as the Gaza Strip. (According to the FBI's most recent statistics, citizens of Chester have a 1-in-18 chance of being the victim of a crime.)

Wisconsin coach Bo Ryan graduated from Chester. So did the Mavericks' Jameer Nelson and McDonald's All-American and Arizona sophomore Rondae Hollis-Jefferson. Tyreke Evans, now of the New Orleans Pelicans, grew up there, although he went to school in a neighboring town.

"I'll never forget: Before we got dressed, one of their players came over and taunted us with a wad of cash," Bryant said. "He flashed $5,000, more money than I'd ever seen in my life, and wanted to bet on the game."

The Spartans and Clippers were about as cordial as the Hatfields and McCoys. When they sized up before tip-off, they might as well have been looking into a mirror. Both squads were fast and physical. They preferred penetrating the lane, pounding the glass, and pressuring the entire length of the floor, all at a breakneck pace. But this season, the Spartans were doing so better than any of the approximately 800 teams in Pennsylvania.

"In the huddle before the game, we said to each other that we were brothers, that we'd stick together out there no matter what happened," Kane said.

"We were one family," Bryant said. "We rode together through it all."

The 32 minutes of action was a battle royal, yielding 30 turnovers, 47 total fouls, four technicals, three ejections, 67 free-throw attempts, and one stunned partisan crowd.

Schenley seized control of a tie game at the dawn of the third quarter, lighting up the scoreboard like a Christmas tree with 54 points in the second half. Kennedy's 26 points and Blair's 23 points, 15 rebounds, and five vicious blocks paced the Spartans in the 85-74 victory. All three of Chester's Division I recruits—juniors Nasir Robinson (Pitt) and Russell Johnson (Robert Morris) and sophomore Rahlir Jefferson (Temple)—watched much of the fourth quarter from the bench, having exhausted their allotment of either personal or technical fouls. The tension remained palpable when the buzzer sounded, as each team retreated to their respective locker rooms without shaking hands.

"There was a lot of jawin' going on out there," Skrocki said. "But that game proved how much of this sport can be mental. The team with the highest basketball I.Q. often wins. Sometimes, you have to give up two easy points, because you can't try to block everything. We were the ones who kept our poise."

The midseason meeting served as a harbinger of the madness to come in March.

After the calendar flipped to February, Schenley tucked another marquee win under its belt, outlasting Maryland's DeMatha Catholic, one of the premier programs in America, by the same margin, 85-74. In the Prime Time Shootout in Trenton, N.J., the Spartans erased a fourth-quarter deficit with a 16-3 run down the stretch. Blair packaged 32 points, 20 boards, five blocks, and five steals, outshining DeMatha's Georgetown signee, Austin Freeman (23 points).

Once the PIAA playoffs began, the pole-positioned Spartans vanquished three straight opponents from the WPIAL—the Western Pennsylvania Interscholastic Athletic League, a conglomeration of more than 100 schools, many well-heeled, in the Pittsburgh suburbs—by an average of 25 points.

In the quarterfinals against Moon and junior guard Brian Walsh, who, six years later, would lead Akron to the NCAA Tournament, DeJuan Blair and Kane shot a combined 16-for-19 from the floor. Their 37 points offset Walsh's 28 points for Moon, the alma mater of Kentucky coach John Calipari. Greg Blair chipped in with 15 points and went 3-for-5 from beyond the arc.

"I don't know who beats them if they shoot the ball this way," Tigers coach Jeff Ackermann said after the 73-59 decision at Duquesne's Palumbo Center. "I don't know what small-college team beats them if they shoot like that. As big as they are and as athletic as they are, I don't know where you stop them offensively."

The Spartans waltzed into their rematch of the previous year's PIAA semifinals with Harrisburg, a school that owned a pair of state crowns (1998 and 2002) that weren't even 10 years old. Although their lineup consisted of Alphonso Dawson (Delaware), Ricardo Brown (Towson), Quincy Roberts (Grambling), and Cameron Artis-Payne, later a running back at Auburn, the Cougars were immediately read their last rites in front of the capacity crowd in Altoona. Schenley shot a scorching 73 percent from the floor, including 7 of 11 from downtown.

"We felt no pressure at all," said DeJuan Blair, who charmed the fans with 19 points and a gamut of emphatic dunks. "That's how confident we were."

Kane drained jumper after jumper as if they were gimme putts on a golf course, scoring a game-high 23 points in the 85-62 rout. Kennedy, meanwhile, had 19 and Greg Blair 15. It was the kind of balance indicative of the way they had shared the ball all winter. (To illustrate that chemistry, Kennedy checked in at 17.2 points per outing by season's end, with DeJuan Blair at 16.2, and Kane at 14.9.)

Awaiting Schenley at the finish line, this time at Penn State's Bryce Jordan Center, was Chester. It was only fitting, since all paths to the promised land in Pennsylvania scholastic basketball run through the almighty Goliath. As Chester discovered two months before, though, Schenley was no David. And it certainly had more than just a slingshot in its arsenal.

As the two heavyweights took the floor to warm up, posturing and primping for the fans, an altercation ensued at half court. Thumping their chests and flexing their muscles, the players from both sides had to be separated by officials and coaches. The stage was set for an epic showdown.

The game, however, was anticlimactic. The Spartans drew first blood and felt little resistance in accomplishing what they began dreaming of the first time they stepped on the blacktop at Kennard Park.

"One of my favorite memories as a sportswriter was at halftime of that game," White said. "When the horn went off, Schenley was up by 11. DeJuan ran the length of the floor along press row, and stopped right in front of me. He glanced around for a few seconds with a deadpan look on his face. Then he grinned and said, 'We gonna win this shit!'"

Correct.

The Spartans sank the Clippers, who never threatened Schenley's comfort while trailing by three possessions for most of the night. As the final seconds ticked off the clock, the margin was 78-71, and the Spartans had claimed their first—and ultimately last—state crown since Jimmy Carter was president.

Kane had 21 points, further cementing how his scholastic career had come full circle with another year to go before graduation. Kennedy was a pristine 10-for-10 from the free-throw line in packaging a double-double (16 points, 11 rebounds).

"It didn't matter if the game looked rough at times," said DeJuan Blair, who was his usual dominant self, tallying 18 points, 23 boards, and six blocks. "We knew it wouldn't look crisp like maybe we wanted it to, but we didn't care. It was a dogfight, and we

Courtesy of Eric Hartline
Chester's Nasir Robinson guards D.J. Kennedy in the 2007 PIAA championship game.

always showed up for a fight. Didn't matter if we won by 100 or 1.

"We were on top of the hill."

Certainly, the pun was intended.

"We wanted immortal status, and I think we got it," he added. "Ten, 20 years from now, people in Pittsburgh will be telling their kids about us. They'll remember the DeJuan Blairs and the D.J. Kennedys and Greg and Jamaal and DeAndre."

"After we won, I sat on the bench and tried to soak it all in, but I didn't really know how to feel,"

Courtesy of Eric Hartline
DeJuan Blair shows his emotion with the outcome of the state final in hand.

said Bryant. "When I walked back to the locker room is when it hit me. I just broke down. DeJuan had just gotten through an interview, and he came and embraced me. I could see the tears in his eyes. I think everyone said 'I love you' something like 15 times."

Not many teams have ever had the luxury of writing Chester's epitaph, but Schenley did it twice in one season.

"What motivated a lot of us was all the old heads in town," Greg Blair said. "They kept saying that we were good, but not that good. Not as good as the other Schenley teams that won state titles. We had to show them."

Blair and company added their names to the pantheon of Spartan legends. And Skrocki, whose hire was once treated with skepticism, finally engraved his name in the history books alongside Willard Fisher, Spencer Watkins, and Fred Yee, whose coaching regimes at Schenley all bore PIAA championships.

X. All that Glitters Isn't Gold

USA TODAY RANKED SCHENLEY 11th in its final Super 25 for the 2006-07 season. Pretty good for a team with only homegrown talent. Which "high school" won the so-called national championship? Duh, Oak Hill. The Warriors played 41 games, exactly half of an NBA schedule, losing just once. Led by Duke recruit Nolan Smith, Oak Hill dispatched of nine state champions along the way. N-I-N-E. Two other schools that finished in the top five—Florida's Montverde Academy and St. Benedict's of Newark, N.J.—also didn't compete for their respective state prizes. Ranking private schools along with public schools, *USA Today* doesn't hesitate to compare apples to oranges.

Montverde Academy, located on the outskirts of Orlando, went 30-0 thanks to five Division I recruits, three of whom hailed from Nigeria or the Ivory Coast with surnames of Alabi, Katuka, and Yotio. Basketball without borders, indeed. Four years prior to that season, in 2002-03, the Eagles didn't win a single game. Not one. By the 2007-08 season, the program had its own media guide with an ad from Nike.

"Our interest in basketball is great, and I don't apologize for that," Montverde Academy headmaster Kasey Kesselring told the *Orlando Magazine*. "While I don't want basketball to define us, there's no question that I consider our athletic programs to be an extension of our marketing program. Sports bring an awareness to our school in ways

50

that a debate team or a science program or a math team don't. That's just our society. We're sports crazy. We recognize that here."

The Eagles are somehow members of the Florida High School Athletic Association. Not wanting to answer the inevitable inquiries about recruiting, however, they choose not to enter its state tournament.

"I recognize that I have the ability to attract students from a wider audience than my counterparts in the public school system," Kesselring said, referring to the 65 percent of Montverde's student body who comes from foreign countries. "So that word 'recruit,' we have to quit using that as if it's a bad word. I have to recruit students here. If a private school doesn't recruit students, then our doors are closed."

St. Benedict's lost just one game that winter, as 6-5 guard Corey Stokes (Villanova) and 6-9 forward Samardo Samuels (Louisville) were practically unstoppable. Samuels arrived in North Jersey from Jamaica, not the neighborhood in nearby Queens but the island in the Caribbean, where he spent the first 14 years of his life.

Less than half of the teams ranked in the Super 25 that season—12 to be exact—were from public schools, and Schenley's company couldn't have been more exclusive. Derrick Rose (Simeon/Chicago), Patrick Patterson (Huntington/W.Va.), James Harden (Artesia/Calif.), Al-Farouq Aminu (Norcross/Ga.), Kyle Singler (South Medford/Ore.), Draymond Green (Saginaw/Mich.), MarShon Brooks (Tucker/Ga.), and Kevin Jones (Mount Vernon/N.Y.) ignored overtures to attend high school elsewhere and performed for the communities that incubated their million-dollar skills.

XI. Giving Back

CHARLIE BATCH CAME OF AGE in Homestead, a few minutes outside Pittsburgh, directly across the Monongahela River from the city line. Before the Steel Valley High School graduate commanded huddles for 14 years as an NFL quarterback for the Lions and Steelers, tragedy struck his family and gave his life a new purpose.

In 1996, as a student at Eastern Michigan, Batch received the news that his 17-year-old sister, Danyl Settles, was slain in the streets of their hometown. Shot once in the head, she was the innocent victim of gangs warring over turf in the small town. Settles was the first of seven people to die in Homestead in just 20 days. The other victims were males in their late teens to late 20s. Though some people claim to know who was responsible for Settles's death, no one has paid the price for it, due to what an Allegheny County judge called sloppy police work.

Three years after his sister's killing, and during his second season as a starter in Detroit, Batch created the Best of the Batch Foundation to help kids in the Pittsburgh area's distressed communities. Providing hope to underprivileged kids through education and sports, he soon discovered, gave him more pleasure than any of the 61 touchdown passes he threw in the NFL.

"I came to a point where I wanted to do whatever I could to prevent the heartbreak that I experienced from losing my sister," said Batch, who won two Super Bowls as a backup with the Steelers. "I know we can't save everybody, but if we save just one, that's one more than we saved yesterday."

Fifteen years old and running as strong as ever, his non-profit functions on the efforts of 100 volunteers. Batch even gives his cell phone number to the children who pass through his programs.

One of them was DeJuan Blair.

Blair—along with some of his teammates, as well as Aliquippa's Herb Pope and Jeannette's Terrelle Pryor—participated in Batch's summer basketball league. Blair developed a relationship with Batch and eventually wrote the foundation a check for the pair of backboards he broke as a youngster.

> "These were true inner-city kids who did things by the book. I understood the struggles they went through, the distractions they avoided."
>
> **—Charlie Batch**

What makes Batch even more relevant to this story was his largess when administrators at Schenley decided the school couldn't afford to purchase rings to commemorate the Spartans' first state title in 29 years.

"It bothered me when the school said they weren't going to pull from their budget to buy the boys rings," he said. "A lot of them came through my foundation. I mean, these were true inner-city kids who did things by the book. I understood the struggles they went through, the distractions they avoided. They did it the right way."

With no parade through The Hill, no banquet to honor their feats, Batch bought the boys their jewelry.

"They were doing fundraisers to try to get the money, but I knew they'd never get enough," he said. "So I called the coach and asked him what it was going to take to get the rings. He gave me the cost, and I told him he'd have the money, but to not let anyone know where it came from.

"The school didn't keep the secret for long though."

In perhaps a sign of the apocalypse, the benevolence of the Best of the Batch Foundation eventually landed on the NCAA's radar.

"I sat down with their representatives for three hours," Batch said. "They weren't concerned with what we were doing for the Division II kids or the NAIA athletes. They only cared about what I was doing for the Division I kids.

"By the end of our meeting, they were almost apologetic. They had no idea how much of an asset we are to our community."

Almost 20 years after his sister's death, her spirit lives on.

"She's remembered," Batch said. "A lot of kids know her face."

XII. Dying a Slow Death

A S THE SPARTANS CELEBRATED their triumph that March evening in Happy Valley, popping bottles of non-alcoholic grape juice and spraying anyone that was somehow still dry in the locker room, the school's obituary was slowly being written.

In a year, the Pittsburgh school board would vote, 5-4, to close Schenley after receiving estimates of between $42 million and $87 million to renovate the building by fixing issues with asbestos and falling plaster.

"Our conclusion, as much as we are pained, is that we value and love the facility but we cannot afford to renovate it," said superintendent Mark Roosevelt. "Our obligation is to better educate this and future generations of our children without saddling Pittsburghers with excessive debt that is not affordable."

Board member Mark Brentley Sr. was one of the dissenting votes. "In the middle of a crisis," he said, "the poor and African-American children are always left out."

The school would die a slow death, as the underclassmen during 2007-08 were moved to the Reizenstein Middle School in East Liberty until the last students to graduate with Schenley on their diploma were sent into the world in June 2011. During that span, almost 75 percent of Schenley's students were minorities and more than 50 percent received free lunch. Its sports programs existed on life support, as they got their younger athletes by way of a cooperative sponsorship with three other schools in the city.

The Jeron Grayson Foundation provided scholarships to seven seniors from the last class of Schenley graduates. Seven recipients were chosen because that was Jeron's jersey number in football.

"Since my children went to Schenley, I found it to be quite a unique and culturally diverse school," said Rev. Grayson. "Even though it did not start out that way, over the years it became diverse."

"My niece was a part of one of the last classes at Schenley," said Darrick Suber. "I went to her graduation, and when it was time for the superintendent to speak, the crowd booed the hell out of him.

"That pretty much summed up how everyone felt when the decision was made to shut down the school. It was gut-wrenching. Schenley was the source of a lot of aspirations, and closing it left a hole that can never be filled."

Jake Oresick, a lawyer and 2001 Schenley graduate who is penning a comprehensive history of the school, clarified the collective ire of generations of Spartans in a June 2008 editorial in the *Post-Gazette*.

"Schenley was exceptional for having defied every traditional paradigm," Oresick wrote. "It transformed racial chasms into a veritable model of socio-economic and cultural fusion. But its most remarkable trait was the way people treated each other. It's about the social boundaries that collapse when a senior class elects a mentally-handicapped student prom queen. It's about the accident of young people connecting—the popular with the petrified, gays with gangsters, Cranberry Township with the Crawford Square projects—and never ever being the same again.

"We all just sort of sat together at the same lunch table."

Pittsburgh's head count, almost 700,000 in the 1960s, has been more than halved, as scarcely 300,000 people now call the city home. The collapse of the steel industry has no doubt been the impetus behind such an exodus. But Pittsburgh's economy has still prospered, as it has transitioned from its industrial heritage to a market buoyed by the new-age moneymakers of health care, finance, and technology. (The University of Pittsburgh Medical Center employs 48,000 people.) However, such white-collar jobs only widen the gap between the haves and have-nots. Many who work in those fields don't reside in the city, but live scattered throughout the affluent suburbs of Mt. Lebanon, Peters Township, Upper St. Clair, Fox Chapel, and Shaler Township.

In addition to Schenley, three other high schools—Peabody, Oliver, and Langley—have recently kicked the bucket, as the district continues its scramble to adjust to its dwindling enrollment. (Since 2004, the district spent more than $23 million on capital improvements to 20 buildings that no longer house students. "Schools are a big investment," said Linda Lane, who succeeded Roosevelt as superintendent in 2011. "You take care of your assets; you just don't let them deteriorate and fall apart because you may not be using them forever.")

Peabody (1911-2011) in East Liberty operated for exactly 100 years before being placed on the chopping block. Its alumni include Hollywood star Gene Kelly, actor Charles Grodin, and writer John Edgar Wideman. Oliver, built in 1925 for 1,700 students, closed in 2012 with about 300 students occupying the North Side school. And Langley, constructed in Pittsburgh's West End in 1923, had the capacity for 1,260 students, but graduated only 123 in its Class of 2012. By the end, all three schools had dropout rates of more than 45 percent.

Now, there are just as many colleges in Pittsburgh as there are public high schools. And the shrinking City League—13 schools deep in its halcyon days—barely has a pulse with Allderdice, Brashear, Carrick, Perry, and Westinghouse still fighting for survival. The newest incarnation of the Pittsburgh Public Schools, the Barack Obama Academy of International Studies, was established in 2009 and is now located in the former Peabody building.

The most positive development amidst this cataclysm is the Pittsburgh Promise. In December 2006, Roosevelt and Luke Ravenstahl—the newly appointed, 26-year-old mayor of Pittsburgh—announced an initiative that would make available to all high school graduates who satisfied the criteria a scholarship of up to $40,000 ($10,000 per year) to any college in Pennsylvania. Since there was no money in place for the Promise at the time, it was a roll of the dice for Ravenstahl, a maverick politician whose time in office was marked by taking risks. The program went into effect two years later, and received its funding through the charitable donations of civic-minded companies like UPMC, which has forked over $100 million to date.

In order to meet the requirements for the Promise, each student must be enrolled at a Pittsburgh Public School for four years and have a minimum attendance record of 90 percent and a GPA of 2.5 or higher.

Ravenstahl dubbed the Promise "a college access program, as well as a revitalization strategy" for Pittsburgh. "I'm confident that families, middle-income families, and families that value education will move into the city when we have this up and running," he said.

"What we're saying to kids in the Pittsburgh Public Schools," said Roosevelt, "is if you play by the rules, and you do what you're supposed to do, and you do your work, and you graduate, there will be education after high school in your future. And money will not be what holds you back."

Jahmiah Guillory, who grew up in the public-housing community of Northview Heights, is the poster child for the Pittsburgh Promise. At the end of the 20th century, studies had shown that residents of the North Side projects where he lived had owned a total of 125 cars, but an average of 3,000 cars were seen entering and exiting each day. Guillory's home, to be frank, was an open-air drug market. It was a place where a lost driver once stopped at a stop sign to ask for directions and was pulled out of her car and beaten by four men, while 20 others watched.

The second of eight children, Guillory worked two jobs to help provide for his family, but he often bagged classes to shoot dice with his friends. Thus, he began his senior year at Oliver with a 1.7 GPA. After hearing about the Promise, Guillory started seeing a tutor at Carnegie Mellon University, and he earned all A's before graduating from Oliver in 2009 to become eligible for a scholarship.

Four years later, he received a bachelor's degree in Petroleum and Natural Gas Engineering from Penn State.

"A lot of people think because you're from the housing projects, you can't be successful," Guillory said. "You have to a drug dealer, a ballplayer, or a rapper. Hopefully, I've shown people that there's another way out."

XIII. Moving On

FOUR MONTHS AFTER shepherding the program to its fifth state title, Skrocki, who always tried to elude the glare of both his supporters and detractors when leaving the gym, slipped out the back door one last time. But in this instance, he was noticed. He stepped down in July 2007 after 24 seasons and 449 wins, none greater than the last. He accepted the coaching position at Butler County Community College, a school five minutes from his house in Jefferson Township, but lasted only three nondescript seasons.

"That wasn't a real program," Skrocki said. "There are 4,000 kids in the school, but I only had seven players, and none of them were taller than 6-2. We never had enough to even scrimmage in practice.

"At Schenley, I once had 80 kids come out for the team, and they couldn't wait to play. At Butler, it was a lot different."

Kevin Reid, a social-studies teacher at Schenley since 1997, inherited the reins from Skrocki for the program's last four years of existence. Reid amassed a 17-76 record in the previous four seasons as the coach at Westinghouse. But going from worst to first came with a caveat, since Schenley was diagnosed as terminal.

"We wanted to go out with a touch of class and have the same type of guts and determination to win as the previous teams," said Reid, a 1982 graduate of Peabody who now teaches civics, anthropology, and African-American history at Perry. "And the kids did that. They showed what I like to call that Schenley gumption, and they wore those jerseys with pride.

"But there was a lot of anxiety and stress among the faculty. For most teachers, it wasn't a question of if they'd be working once the school closed, but where. Overall, there was just a lingering sense of sadness."

> "A lot of people say, 'Well, Schenley used to win by 20, 40.' Well those days are gone."
>
> **—Kevin Reid**

Initially for Reid, the cupboard was hardly bare, as Kane and Greg Blair returned in 2007-08 and led the Spartans to their fourth consecutive City League crown. Kane averaged a whopping 31.1 points per game, but Schenley bowed out of the PIAA tournament in the first round to McKeesport and its 6-11 junior, Zeke Marshall (Akron).

"A lot of people say, 'Well, Schenley used to win by 20, 40,'" Reid told the *Tribune-Review* after the loss. "Well those days are gone."

Forever.

XIV. Father Time Catches Up

SCHENLEY ALMOST REACHED its centennial, but in the end, it died of natural causes, falling victim to age and progress. Several of the school's hardwood stars, though, weren't as fortunate as their alma mater and took their last breaths much too soon.

Sonny Lewis, who could elevate as if unencumbered by gravity, oddly died in April 1981 at the tender age of 23. His mother found his lifeless body in bed the morning after he played pickup at Duquesne. At the time, he was entertaining an offer to play in Venezuela. Toxicology tests revealed that Lewis had an unidentified drug in his system.

"We've never seen it before," said Chief Toxicologist Dr. Charles Winek. "We don't have any known, pure standards of every illegally made drug."

The autopsy showed no indications that Lewis was a narcotics user, and the coroner ruled his death was caused by a reaction "to an unknown drug."

Western Pennsylvania native John Clayton, now an NFL reporter at ESPN, began his writing career at the *Pittsburgh Press*. He eloquently captured the vibe on The Hill's streets the day Lewis died.

"A cold wind whipped through the Hill District yesterday," Clayton wrote. "Early morning rain was replaced by late afternoon chill, but no rainbow was in sight. Around the world, a space shuttle landed in California. National leaders regrouped around a wounded president. Polish workers, forever fearing the threat of the Soviet Union, rationed a dwindling supply of food. Yet The Hill remains insulated from much of the outside world. Residents there endure their own realities. The stock market may rise or fall, but poverty remains constant. Astronauts orbit the earth, but food stamps may not buy enough nourishment for a family of six. Crumbled buildings are monuments to the trying times."

Clayton continued: "Lewis's life was not as mysterious as his death. Lewis, like many other schoolyard legends, chased a rainbow, slam-dunking a basketball through a hoop with each step. Many have followed the rainbow-like flight of basketball out of ghettos and into riches. Sonny never found his pot of gold."

Kenny Durrett passed away from a heart attack in January 2001, one month after turning 52. He was a community activist and moved to Wilkinsburg in the suburbs, and coached the girls at the local high school.

"I saw Ken Durrett, and I knew he was going to be a better player than I was," Tom Gola once told the *Philadelphia Inquirer*. The Naismith Hall of Famer and fabled Explorer coached Durrett for two years at La Salle. "He had all the moves before Dr. J. He had that shooting range, and that fluid motion going to the basket."

"Kenny had every ingredient: size, skill, you name it," said Temple coach Fran Dunphy, Durrett's teammate in college. "We knew he wasn't 100 percent when he got to the NBA. That was tragic. It was a shame he was never able to come back from his knee injury."

Jeep Kelley, Lewis's kin, died of cardiac arrest at the age of 54 in March 2008. He drove a bus and worked with youths at clinics, camps, and rec centers.

"When he took his physical at UNLV as a freshman, he was diagnosed as suffering from malnutrition," said Tony Morocco, the coach at Seton Hill University and Kelley's longtime friend. "On every level when you talk about him, the word 'unfortunate' is used. He never had the same bed to sleep in as a child, and everything around him was unstable. He didn't have positive things to gravitate to."

Maurice Lucas saw his 58th birthday before succumbing to bladder cancer in 2010. He lived in Oregon and was an assistant coach with the Trail Blazers. The team honored him by wearing patches with his No. 20 on their jerseys during the 2010-11 season.

"In all my years, I've never met someone who was so strong," Sonny Vaccaro told the *Post-Gazette* after Lucas's death. "He was a proud son of a gun who knew one day he'd get out of The Hill. His mindset was different. He wasn't a typical city kid. The Hill was tough, and it was tough to get out of there. But Maurice, you sort of knew he would get out.

"He had goals. Of all the kids I've been around, I knew he would be one of the ones to get through all the bull. He died too young, but at least he was able to get out and make it to the top."

Calvin Kane died of a brain aneurysm in 2012 at the age of 50. He had once run with a troubled crowd and spent a year in prison, but he was on the right side of the law when he collapsed in The Hill and was subsequently taken off life support.

"I played every day at the Franklin Street projects," Darrick Suber said about his youth in the 1980s when cocaine was tearing through inner-cities like a tornado. "I was fortunate enough to have Jeep and Calvin take a liking to me. They saw the passion I had for the game and became my mentors. They gave me protection, an instant insulation from their woes and the dark paths that a lot of guys traveled down."

Now, Suber couldn't be farther from The Hill and its despair. He lives in suburban Seattle and works in online advertising and consulting. His clients include mammoth brands like Microsoft, Nike, Red Bull, and the Bleacher Report.

It's a strange coincidence that Lewis, Durrett, Kelley, Lucas, and Kane—a starting five for the ages—never made it to retirement. Larry Anderson, for one, doesn't have to be reminded of that fact.

"I went to Sonny's and Maurice's funerals," said Anderson, who remained in Las Vegas after his days as a Rebel and started 3-Point Tequila, a basketball-themed spirit with his silhouette on the bottle. "I didn't make it back home when Calvin passed. It's probably a good thing, too. It would've been too overwhelming. I had just spoken with him two weeks before he died.

"I guess it's a part of life that when you get older, you have to bury your friends. But it doesn't get easier over time."

XV. DeJuan Blair

ALTHOUGH THEIR SCHOOL has gone belly up, the hoop dreams of DeJuan Blair, D.J. Kennedy, and DeAndre Kane are alive and well.

With the Petersen Events Center only a few football fields from his house, Blair chose Pitt over Tennessee and its charismatic coach Bruce Pearl, who would drop by The Hill at a moment's notice during his recruitment. Blair became the first City League player to wear the blue and gold in the 16 years since Perry's Darelle Porter graduated in 1991.

"When I recruited him at Schenley, it was almost comical the way he dominated," said former Pitt assistant coach Mike Rice. "He'd be boxing out, all perfectly legal, and get called for fouls because kids would fall down, and the refs would feel sorry for them."

As a sophomore in 2008-09, Blair shared the Big East Player of the Year Award with Connecticut's Hasheem Thabeet, and was a consensus first-team All-American alongside James Harden, Stephen Curry, Blake Griffin, and Tyler Hansbrough. Not bad company for the big fella. He led the Panthers to the Elite Eight, and soon declared for the NBA draft.

"I told him from the time I recruited him that I always thought he was an NBA player," said Pitt coach Jamie Dixon. "I've always had a higher opinion of him than most scouting services and coaches and most media observers."

In the months leading up to the draft, Blair trimmed his body fat from 16 percent down to 9.7 percent. Expecting to be a first-round pick with a guaranteed contract, he instead waited three hours for his name to be called on draft night. After tests revealed the lack of an ACL in each knee, his stock plummeted due to concerns about their durability. (Blair's doctors purposefully did not remove the ligaments when he injured them, but over time, they deteriorated to the point of disappearance.) The Spurs snatched him up early in the second round, where draftees are promised nothing.

Courtesy of the University of Pittsburgh
It only took two years for DeJuan Blair to become an All-American at Pitt.

"It's been a while since draft night, and I remember it like it was yesterday," Blair said. "My brother and I were watching together, and [NBA commissioner] David Stern kept coming up to the podium and announcing the names of guys I knew I was better than.

"By the 23rd or 24th pick, I was so fed up that I went into another room and hit the weights. Every time I was passed up, I'd lift a different weight until the Spurs took me at 37. And all the anxiety and frustration were gone."

Although Blair played in every game before January 13, 2010 as a rookie for San Antonio, defying the odds against a second-round pick even making a roster, his minutes were sparse until that night. Spurs coach Gregg Popovich decided it was time to rest Tim Duncan, his aging superstar, against the Thunder at Chesapeake Energy Arena in Oklahoma City. He inserted Blair into the starting lineup, and Blair collected 28 points and 21 rebounds in 31 minutes before fouling out in overtime of San Antonio's 109-108 victory.

"I'm going to take what he gave us tonight, and I don't know how he did it," Popovich told *The Associated Press*. "I have no clue what his moves are. He's just a basketball player. He hustles his [tail] off, he's got a nose for the ball, he's got great hands, and he does what you saw. We didn't teach him any of it. He brought it all with him."

Three months later in Dallas, on April 14, the last night of the regular season, Blair was again a bull in a china shop. With Duncan and Manu Ginobili resting, Blair had 27 points, 23 boards, four assists, and three steals in a 96-89 loss to the Mavericks.

Both outings confirmed that this second-rounder was in the NBA to stay. As a power forward who is somewhat limited by his size, Blair is most often compared to Elton Brand. However, a more accurate parallel might be Danny Fortson. With a rugged build akin to Blair's and the 6-7 height to match, Fortson was also the last player from Western Pennsylvania to compete in the NBA before Blair. (The Altoona native once detonated a 60-point, 21-rebound bomb in a game as a high school sophomore. A tumultuous childhood—one that involved an alcoholic and abusive father, depressed mother, and a sister who killed her boyfriend—compelled Fortson to move in with his

© *John Albright/San Antonio Express-News/*
ZUMA Wire
Motivated by the disappointment of being passed over in the first round of the 2009 NBA draft, DeJuan Blair broke out as a rookie for the San Antonio Spurs.

grandmother and finish his scholastic career at Shaler, just minutes north of Pittsburgh.) Fortson left Cincinnati as a junior and played a decade in the league, and his statistics are strikingly similar to Blair's.

Now in his sixth NBA season, Blair, who was peerless in the paint in high school, is an energy guy in the pros, having to square off with opponents four to five inches taller than him. Offensively, he uses his hips and leverage well to keep them off balance. And defensively, he has shown how much of an asset he can be as a disruptive force off the bench.

"Putting on for Pittsburgh is awesome," he said. "I learned so much when I was 14, 15 going against grown men at Kennard Park. Heart beats out height—that lesson has served me well in the NBA. Some guys are scared to get their shot blocked, so they're tentative, but not me. They key is playing every play like it's my last."

Blair's prior contracts have been short in length and at or near the minimum salary for someone of his service. His most recent one, though, with the Washington Wizards is a multi-year deal that will fatten his pockets to the tune of $6 million over three seasons.

"When I first tore my ACL in high school, I *thought* I was done," Blair said. "Then I did it again, and I *knew* I was done.

"I've been blessed, really. I'm accustomed to my life as a professional basketball player now, but periodically, it'll hit me out of nowhere, how lucky I am. And I'll thank God for what I've been given."

"DeJuan will always be loved in Pittsburgh," Mike White said. "It's his attitude. He's genuine, always smiling on and off the court. I remember when we had him come to our office to get his picture taken when he was a senior. He had on a Schenley state-championship t-shirt. I told him I needed to get one of them, and he said, 'Here, have mine.' And he started taking it off, before I stopped him.

"That's the kind of guy he is—willing to give you the shirt off his back."

XVI. D.J. Kennedy

T HE GAME BETWEEN the Wizards and host Cleveland Cavaliers on April 25, 2012 at Quicken Loans Arena was a matchup of two teams going nowhere. Both franchises were playing out the string of yet another campaign of rebuilding. It appeared that most players were just going through the motions, even though the end of that lockout-shortened season seemed to arrive with more haste than usual. The game—billed as a duel between point guards John Wall and Kyrie Irving, the top picks in the previous two drafts—was Cleveland's home finale at The Q and drew 18,086 customers. It was proof that although the Cavs were incapable of winning without King James, they could still fill their arena during the four years his talents were in South Beach.

Of the fans in attendance, it would've taken one with extreme knowledge to understand the night's significance to D.J. Kennedy. One year before, in the twilight of his spectacular career at St. John's, he shredded his knee in the Big East quarterfinals and was unable to play in the Red Storm's first NCAA Tournament game in nine seasons.

"St. John's got so much love from New York in the [Madison Square] Garden that it's impossible to put into words," said David Kennedy Sr. "The atmosphere was electric. I went to almost every home game when D.J. was a senior. They knocked off three Top 10 teams there—Duke,

UConn, and Pitt. We all felt they were going to make a deep tournament run. Until D.J. got hurt.

"You could hear a pin drop in the Garden. The pain on his face told the whole story."

Slated to be a second-round pick, Kennedy went undrafted and endured an intense rehab to get ready for his impending stint with the D-League's Erie BayHawks. His numbers in Erie—15.7 points, 7.3 rebounds, and 4.4 assists in 44 games—warranted a promotion to the Cavs with two games left in their season.

Kennedy's mother, father, stepfather, and sister made the two-hour drive from Pittsburgh to

Courtesy of St. John's University
D.J. Kennedy was instrumental in putting the Red Storm back on the basketball map.

Cleveland and waited anxiously, wondering if he would even get into the game. They didn't have to wait long. With 3:51 left in the first quarter, Cavs coach Byron Scott summoned Kennedy off the bench. Despite the butterflies in his stomach, Kennedy felt light on his feet when he checked in for Anthony Parker. Two minutes and 27 seconds later, he let fly his first shot as an NBA player, sinking a trey from 25 feet to give the Cavs a four-point lead. From then on, Kennedy did what he's always done since he first bounced a ball in The Hill.

© *USA Today Sports Images. Reprinted with permission.*
D.J. Kennedy's reward for an excellent 2011-12 season in the
D-League was a call-up to the Cleveland Cavaliers.

He stuffed the stat sheet.

Irving, plagued by the flu, only logged 10 minutes in Cleveland's 96-85 loss, but Kennedy helped fill the void in the backcourt. He tallied 12 points, six boards, three assists, and two steals in 31 minutes as the Cavs' top performer.

"That was a beautiful moment," said Kennedy Sr. "Just seeing what D.J. put himself through in rehab to get back out there. Man, it made me so proud.

"Dallas drafted me the same year [1981] as Mark Aguirre and Rolando Blackman, so I never really had a chance to make the team. The writing was on the wall when I went to camp. But D.J. made it, and no one can take that away from him."

The next day, Cleveland traveled to Chicago, where Kennedy went scoreless in a 32-point loss to the Bulls. He was in the NBA for less than a week, and as the years pass, he remains a long shot to return. If he doesn't, he'll be basketball's version of Moonlight Graham.

"There are a lot of guys out there who are good enough to be in the league," D.J. said. "The timing and situation have to be right, though, in order for you to stick around. If anything, I think I proved I belong. If I don't make it back, then so be it. I'm just going to keep doing what I'm doing."

Kennedy played the majority of the next year with the BayHawks before being traded to the Rio Grande Valley Vipers with a month left in the season. His 21.3 points, 9.3 rebounds, 6.0 assists, and 2.2 steals in the playoffs catapulted the Texas franchise to its second D-League championship.

Now pursuing bigger paychecks in foreign lands, Kennedy signed with a Russian club for the 2014-15 season, and in doing so, reunited with a familiar face across the globe.

XVII. Jamaal Bryant

NEARBY PROGRAMS West Virginia and Duquesne found Jamaal Bryant appealing as a senior at Schenley. But he didn't make the grade coming out of high school, and was thus relegated to the netherworld of college basketball.

On the recommendation of newly appointed Mountaineers coach Bob Huggins, Onion spent the 2007-08 season at Broward Community College in Fort Lauderdale. There, he showed glimpses of what might have been, like his 30 points, seven rebounds, nine assists, and nine steals against the College of the Bahamas.

"Bob called me, and said 'I got a midget or a seven-footer for you, but the midget can really play,'" said Broward coach Bob Starkman, a native New Yorker with an accent as thick as a slice of cheesecake. "I told him I'd take the midget. Not many college basketball coaches turn down a seven-footer, but I did.

"It worked out well for a while, but he left school after the season was over. Before he got his credits for the second semester."

"I lived in an apartment down there, and went home to Pittsburgh one time in April," Bryant said. "When I got back, we had no electricity, because my roommate didn't pay the bill. With no air conditioning in Florida, it gets sticky, and I wasn't going to live like that."

His next stop was Barstow Community College in Southern California, but a disagreement with the coach's son sent him home earlier than expected. Then came Marshalltown Community College in Iowa, where he never got the chance to play because he didn't fill out some necessary paperwork.

"Junior college was a grind," Bryant said. "Some of those places don't really have campuses or cafeterias, and you live in an apartment and are responsible for all your meals. It's not like I had family back in Pittsburgh sending me money. And when I came home, I wasn't really pushed to go back."

Deflated emotionally and with the curtain coming down on his basketball being, Onion moved to San Antonio for a few months to room with Blair in one of Tony Parker's properties.

"A lot of people have their hands out, but I didn't expect nothing from DeJuan," he said. "I just wanted to experience the NBA lifestyle because I knew that's as close I was ever going to get. We were in a gated community, and partied when we could, but it's not what a lot of people think it is. I got my mind right down there."

Now, Bryant works for a non-profit, violence-prevention program in Pittsburgh. And nary a day goes by when he doesn't think about his time as a Spartan.

XVIII. DeAndre Kane

DEANDRE KANE TOOK a more circuitous route to the cusp of the NBA. He prepped for a year at The Patterson School in Lenoir, N.C. before pledging his services to Marshall and redshirting the following season as a partial qualifier.

When he finally began his collegiate career in 2010-11, he hit the ground running and was named the Conference USA Freshman of the Year. In his junior year in Huntington, he recorded the program's fourth-ever triple-double with 33 points, 11 rebounds, and 10 assists against Hofstra. By then, however, he had worn out his welcome with the Thundering Herd, as coach Tom Herrion withdrew Kane's scholarship with one season of eligibility remaining.

As *Sports Illustrated* later reported in February 2014, Kane twice led the nation in technical fouls at Marshall, punched a teammate in the face during a scrimmage, threw a bottle of Gatorade at an undergraduate manager for messing up his food order, and clashed so much with coaches and teammates that an assistant threatened to quit if he wasn't dismissed.

"Marshall tried to make me look bad," he said, "and for no good reason. The city was my second home, and I apologize to the fans who spent their money and cheered their lungs out that we didn't get to the [NCAA] Tournament. They deserved that."

Kane's father's death during his sophomore season had a profound effect on him.

"I had just talked to him two days before he passed," DeAndre said. "We talked like every other day on the phone. I didn't want to play basketball no more. It still hurts to this day. But I came back and dedicated it to him. He wanted me to get to the NBA more than I did. This was his dream."

After becoming the first member of his family to obtain a degree, Kane transferred to Iowa State, a program built with reclamation projects, and closed out his college career in sterling fashion. With norms of 17.1 points, 6.8 rebounds, and

Courtesy of Marshall University
As a sophomore at Marshall, DeAndre Kane once scored 40 points in a triple-overtime victory over Tulsa in the Conference USA quarterfinals.

5.9 assists, he joined lottery picks Andrew Wiggins and Marcus Smart on the All-Big 12 First Team and led the Cyclones to the Sweet 16.

"DeAndre took accountability for his past," Iowa State coach Fred Hoiberg said. "If he would've blamed everybody but himself, that would've been a red flag. He talked about how he really learned from what he did in the past, and didn't want to repeat it.

"We didn't have any issues with DeAndre. When you bring a guy in as a transfer, there are so many rumors that go around. But he came right in and fit with our culture. I give him a lot of credit for changing his ways. At least, in terms of what the perception of him was."

Twenty-five at the time of the 2014 Draft, Kane, much like Kennedy three years before him, was an estimate for the second round but was not selected. He participated with the Lakers in the Las Vegas Summer League, and is playing the 2014-15 season alongside Kennedy in Russia.

If an NBA contract isn't in the cards, Kane will continue to

Courtesy of Iowa State University
DeAndre Kane found a nice landing spot with the Cyclones, leading them to the NCAA Tournament's Sweet 16.

make a hefty salary overseas, which is fine by him. He knows that it could have been his chalk outline on the pavement of some dark alley in The Hill.

XIX. Greg Blair

WHEN HE GRADUATED from Schenley in 2008, Greg Blair was still five inches shorter than his brother and thus fully aware that basketball would not be his ticket out of The Hill. He spent a year at North Carolina Tech and two years at Lackawanna Junior College in Scranton, sculpting his body for the rigors of Division I football and morphing into a terror of an inside linebacker. He signed with Cincinnati for what he thought was two years of eligibility, but he was ultimately granted a third by the NCAA.

As a junior in 2012, Blair led the Big East in tackles. His 19 tackles, including two sacks of Teddy Bridgewater, in a narrow loss to Louisville were a career-high. In that season's Belk Bowl in Charlotte, with the Bearcats trailing Duke, 16-3, early in the second quarter, Blair stuffed a running back at the goal line, stripping the Blue Devil and recovering the fumble. The play gave Cincinnati a shot in the arm, much like his exploits on the court did to Schenley, as it scored 24 straight points on the way to a 48-34 victory.

"Cincinnati was perfect for me," Blair said. "It was within driving distance, and a lot of guys on my team had that Pennsylvania-Ohio rivalry in their DNA. We'd always talk smack about who had the better players."

Courtesy of the University of Cincinnati
As a Bearcat, Greg Blair became a menace to opposing quarterbacks in the Big East.

Just like his brother has demonstrated his bona fides as a professional athlete, Greg would like to do the same after not hearing his name called in the 2014 NFL Draft. He attended rookie camp with the Cleveland Browns and got an up-close view of the circus surrounding Johnny Football, but he didn't earn a contract. Blair is hopeful that, somewhere, things will work out.

XX. Perspective Is Everything

WITH ALL THE CHANGES that scholastic hoops have endured, the game has been rendered unrecognizable to most people. Supporting the local kids in their quest for a humbled version of athletic immortality was once the thing to do on Friday nights across America. It transported us back to our carefree days in high school, as if we were swimming in a fountain of youth.

Now, the best "locals" are gone, off chasing opportunities and exposure in environments better suited to groom them for their careers that lie ahead. And no one is stopping them.

Sports are meant to enhance the high school experience, not be the high school experience. Unfortunately, society has turned a corner, and there's no going back to that line of thinking. The direction we're headed in had Allen High School in Texas construct an 18,000-seat football stadium in 2012 for $60 million. High school conferences have preseason media days for football like the power conferences in college. And the rash of transfers in basketball resembles the NBA's free-agent system, as 52 of the Top 100 recruits in the Class of 2013 attended multiple high schools. With sports embedded in our culture for so long, it was only a matter of time before they became more of a business pursuit for teenagers than a recreational one.

If Calvin Kane's NBA dream for his son comes true, DeAndre would be the third player from Schenley's 2006-07 title squad to make the league. You'll have to turn back the clock pretty far to find a public high school team that consisted of as many as three NBA ballers.

In 1981-82, Baltimore's Dunbar High School fit that bill. With David Wingate, Reggie Williams, Muggsy Bogues, and Reggie Lewis, an argument can be made that the 29-0 Poets were the greatest scholastic outfit of all time. Lewis was the only one of these four Poets who did not play at least a decade in the NBA, but that's only because the Celtics' All-Star died on the practice court at the age of 27.

Detroit's now-defunct Southwestern High School finished 28-0 in 1989-90. Before they were drafted, senior Howard Eisley (Boston College) and juniors Jalen Rose (Michigan) and Voshon Lenard (Minnesota) led the Prospectors to their first state title in 17 years.

A year later, in 1990-91, Chicago's Proviso East cut down the nets when the Illinois High School Association still had a two-class system, ensuring that the toughest of competition in America's fifth-most populated state stood in its way. The Pirates went 32-1 and featured Michael Finley (Wisconsin), Donnie Boyce (Colorado), and Sherrell Ford (Illinois-Chicago). Finley was a two-time All-Star with the Mavericks, while Boyce and Ford both had short spells in the league.

Championships are won every year on every level of every sport. All are memorable for the participants, for both those who carried their teams and those whose contributions didn't appear in box scores but were as tangible as points, rebounds, and assists. But not all high school championships are historic, worthy of plaudits beyond their region. How good can the titlists in Wyoming, Vermont, Alaska, North Dakota, and South Dakota actually be, when each has fewer than a million residents yet still crowns multiple state champions? Combined, their populations roughly equal that of Connecticut, which is also smaller than 28 other states.

Championship trophies are now being distributed like candy on Halloween, and with more added into the circulation, their value is diminishing in the eyes of anyone who didn't have a hand in them. Florida and Kansas each crowned eight state champions at the conclusion of the 2013-14 boys basketball season. Louisiana and Oklahoma had seven. California,

> Championship trophies are now being distributed like candy on Halloween.

Washington, Illinois, Virginia, and Georgia had six. Texas, Wisconsin, and Tennessee had five.

Pennsylvania, the sixth-most populated state, only has four classes. Kansas has half as many high schools as Pennsylvania, but it crowns twice as many champions. Given this math, winning a championship in the Keystone State is now as glamorous as ever. Especially for the conventional public schools, the talent pools of which are plundered more with each passing year.

During the 2012-13 school year, the School District of Philadelphia had 28 percent of its students enrolled in charters. Contrast that with Houston's 19 percent, Los Angeles's 18 percent, Miami's 13 percent, Chicago's 12 percent, and New York City's six percent. Then add into the mix Pennsylvania's private schools, especially those in the Philadelphia Catholic League. You can quickly see how rampant recruiting is a nightmare for public schools that dream of being one of Pennsylvania's four champions.

To be fair, public schools all across the country have shown time and again that they aren't immune to cutting corners or selling their souls in exchange for sports glory.

Frederick Douglass High School in Oklahoma City won five straight Class 4A titles from 2011-2014, but an affidavit accusing the principal of tampering with grades and modifying attendance records so the players could maintain their eligibility cast a cloud of suspicion over their success. A 2012 audit of the school revealed that 95 percent of its juniors were not on track to graduate on time.

In 2013-14, Seattle's James Garfield High School, the alma mater of Brandon Roy and Tony Wroten, claimed Washington's Class 4A crown for the first time in 16 years. Six players in the Bulldogs' rotation transferred in from other schools, raising questions about the program's ethics.

And James Madison High School in Dallas was forced to forfeit its back-to-back Class 3A championships in 2013 and 2014 amid a recruiting scandal that came to light after a player's murder over a video game. An investigation determined that the two players lived together yet attended separate schools, for which neither was eligible to compete. When the dust settled after the killing, the Dallas Independent School District fired 15 employees, including athletic directors and coaches who were found to have fabricated student residency documents.

No such pall hung like an anvil over Schenley's achievements.

The Spartans have always epitomized the gritty soul of The Hill and, by extension, the proletarian ethos of a city that never had an NBA team and is, numbers-wise, a shell of its former self. (Although Pittsburgh is the second-largest city in Pennsylvania, California alone has 12 cities with more residents than Pittsburgh.) The school may be extinct, but the mythology of its basketball program survives. The 2006-07 Spartans were as pure as snow, having reached the PIAA's pinnacle untainted by the allegations of impropriety that dog so many elite scholastic programs in the 21st century. DeJuan and Greg Blair, D.J. Kennedy,

Jamaal Bryant, and DeAndre Kane attended Schenley as freshmen, and they graduated from Schenley as seniors. It's a sad commentary on society to say how rare that is today.

"The legend of that Schenley team will only grow over time," Mike White said. "The status of the greatest high school teams is often determined by what the players do after high school. In that regard, those guys were as good as anyone.

"They were the most memorable team I've ever covered in any sport, and I've been doing this [for the *Post-Gazette*] since 1979, for 35 years. A lot of teams win championships despite lacking something. Schenley lacked nothing. They were such a cast of characters, always good-natured, but with just enough craziness to make it interesting. We may never again see a group of kids born and raised in the same neighborhood, like they were, do what they did."

After sitting uninhabited for six years, Schenley will soon be converted into 160 luxury apartments, thus signaling its official end with education. In 2013, the PMC Property Development Group bought the 97-year-old building—its peeled paint, fallen plaster, exposed wiring, buckled flooring and all—for $5.2 million. The Philadelphia-based firm, which owns other properties in Pittsburgh, plans to invest another $37 million in the overhaul. PMC outbid other groups that wanted to open—you guessed it—a charter school. That would've been a crime tantamount to the abuse of a corpse.

For old-school basketball fans, apartments sound like a great idea.

References

"76ers Owner Puts Season in Context." *Associated Press*, April 19, 2014.

Ashe, Braden. "MLK Observance Speaker Talks of 'Dreams and Nightmares.'" *Valley News Dispatch*, January 27, 2014.

Axelrod, Phil. "Obituary: Robert 'Jeep' Kelley, High School Basketball Legend." *Pittsburgh Post-Gazette*, March 16, 2008.

Bailey, Doug. "Arson, Looting Brought under Control: Police, Guard Put Lid on Pittsburgh." *Associated Press*, April 8, 1968.

Baker, Kent. "Poetic Dominance: Dunbar Sets the Standard among Area's All-Time Best." *Baltimore Sun*, February 28, 1995.

Bauder, Bob. "Many Fear Pittsburgh's Hill District Will Never Reach Another Zenith." *Pittsburgh Tribune-Review*, February 23, 2014.

Billson, Marky. "Schenley Stops Oliver in Double Overtime." CoachesAid.com, November 14, 2009.

"Blair Sets Career Highs as Spurs Trump Thunder in Overtime." *Associated Press*, January 13, 2010.

Bowser, Terry. "Court Warfare." *Huntingdon Daily News*. March 20, 1978.

Burnside, Jeff. "Garfield High 'Super Team' Has Six Transfers, Raising Questions." KOMO News, March 3, 2014.

Chang, David. "Philly Teachers to Debut New Ad Attacking Mayor." NBC 10, September 3, 2013.

Chute, Eleanor. "Pittsburgh Promise Scholarship Recipient Defied Odds." *Pittsburgh Post-Gazette*, December 29, 2013.

-----------. "Pittsburgh School District Spent $23 Million on Now-Closed Buildings." *Pittsburgh Post-Gazette*, February 24, 2013.

"Cincinnati Shocks Duke with 83-yard TD Pass with 44 Seconds Left." ESPN.com, December 27, 2012.

Clayton, John. "No Pot of Gold for Sonny Lewis." *Pittsburgh Press*, April 15, 1981.

Cohen, Micah. "St. Benedict's Basketball Plays Two." *New York Times*, January 19, 2007.

"Coroner: Basketball Star Died from Drug." *Pittsburgh Post-Gazette*, July 2, 1981.

Deveney, Sean. "After Long Journey, DeAndre Kane to Honor Father in Draft." *Sporting News*, June 20, 2014.

Dunn, Marcia. "Teachers Go Back to School and Like It." *Associated Press*, May 29, 1984.

Dvorchak, Robert. "From Tragedy, Steelers' Charlie Batch Offers Hope." *Pittsburgh Post-Gazette*, January 3, 2010.

Emert, Rich. "Near Miss: Mark Halsel, Robert Morris Might Have Made Perfect Pair." *Pittsburgh Press*, January 17, 1984.

Enrietto, John. "Small Roster Hurts BC3 Men's Team." *The Cranberry Eagle*, November 18, 2009.

Everett, Brad. "Schenley Slams DeMatha, 85-74." *Pittsburgh Post-Gazette*, February 11, 2007.

Fittipaldo, Ray. "J.O. Stright: The Man in the Middle." *Pittsburgh Post-Gazette*, May 14, 2006.

-----------. "Obituary: Maurice Lucas, Schenley Grad Regarded as 'Best Player to Ever Come out of Pittsburgh.'" *Pittsburgh Post-Gazette*, November 2, 2010.

Forgrave, Reid. "DeAndre Kane Breaks out at Iowa State after Long, Dangerous Journey." FOX Sports, March 3, 2014.

Fox, Randy. "Pittsburgh's Hill District: The Death of a Dream." *Huffington Post*, July 16, 2012.

Fuoco, Michael. "Return to Glory: Hill District Determined to Regain Lost Greatness." *Pittsburgh Post-Gazette*, April 11, 1999.

Gigler, Rich. "Twenty Watch Four Beat Woman Motorist who Got Lost in Northview Heights." *Pittsburgh Press*, November 27, 1990.

Grupp, John. "Blair: Weight Down, Stock up for NBA Draft." *Pittsburgh Tribune-Review*, June 21, 2009.

Gurman, Sadie. "Hill District Pastor's 'Sympathy Has Turned to Empathy.'" *Pittsburgh Post-Gazette*, October 21, 2010.

Haynes, Monica. "MLK Riots: When Patience Ran out, The Hill Went up in Flames." *Pittsburgh Post-Gazette*, April 2, 2008.

Heinz, Frank. "Dallas Madison Forced to Forfeit State Championships amid DISD Recruiting Scandal." NBC 5, August 15, 2014.

Hostutler, Mark. "Carroll Decides not to Leave American Christian Quietly." *Delaware County Daily Times*, June 17, 2006.

-----------. "Chester Can't Catch Schenley." *Delaware County Daily Times*, January 29, 2007.

-----------. *Heads of State: Pennsylvania's Greatest High School Basketball Players of the Modern Era.* Bloomington, IN: iUniverse, Inc., 2010.

Hughes, Debra. "A Threatened Pittsburgh School Becomes a Center for Renewal." *Education Week*, December 1, 1982.

Juliano, Joe. "Ken Durrett: Just How Good Could He Have Been?" *Philadelphia Inquirer*, January 9, 2001.

Kalson, Sally. "Much History will be Lost with Closing of Schenley." *Pittsburgh Post-Gazette*, November 10, 2005.

Katz, Andy. "Marshall's Kane Honors His Father's Memory." ESPN.com, October 24, 2012.

Kerasotis, Peter. "Building a Bigger Giant." *Orlando Magazine*, April 2012.

Lafferty, Tricia. "McKeesport Ousts Schenley from PIAA Playoffs." *Pittsburgh Tribune-Review*, March 2, 2008.

-----------. "Schenley Eases into New Era." *Pittsburgh Tribune-Review*, December 25, 2007.

-----------. "Schenley Player Considers Basketball Talent a Blessing." *Pittsburgh Tribune-Review*, April 8, 2007.

-----------. "Schenley Takes Care of Harrisburg." *Pittsburgh Tribune-Review*, March 22, 2007.

-----------. "Silver Lining not Good Enough for Schenley." *Pittsburgh Tribune-Review*, March 20, 2007.

Lord, Rich. "Tuition Grants a Lure for City Schools." *Pittsburgh Post-Gazette*, December 14, 2006.

"Mavericks Use Early Run to Down Spurs in Preview of Playoffs." *Associated Press*, April 14, 2010.

McLane, Jeff. "Lower Merion Storms back to Win the Crown." *Philadelphia Inquirer*, March 26, 2006.

Monahan, Lisa. "Douglass High May Lose Championship Titles Due to Cheating Allegations." News 9, October 8, 2012.

O'Neil, Dana. "Just a Short Walk from Home, Local Boy Blair Makes Good with Panthers." ESPN.com, January 29, 2009.

Oresick, Jake. "Why We Fight for Schenley: It's a Unique Meeting Place of Cultures Where High School Doesn't Seem Like High School." *Pittsburgh Post-Gazette*, June 25, 2008.

Ove, Torsten. "Monessen Man Arrested in Fatal Shooting Near Cal U Campus." *Pittsburgh Post-Gazette*, October 19, 2010.

Panaccio, Tim. "Schenley Nips Wilkinsburg." *Pittsburgh Post-Gazette*, March 9, 1978.

Patton Smith, Carole. "It's 'Cool to be Smart' Now at Schenley High School." *Pittsburgh Post-Gazette*, February 15, 1988.

-----------. "Schenley Students Learn to Settle Feuds." *Pittsburgh Post-Gazette*, April 4, 1988.

Pitz, Marylynne. "MLK Riots: 40 Years Later, Turmoil on The Hill Stirs Memories." *Pittsburgh Post-Gazette*, April 2, 2008.

Prisbell, Eric. "After Drama, Iowa State's DeAndre Kane Writes Happy Ending." *USA Today*, January 13, 2004.

Pro, Johnna A. "Obituary: Ken Durrett, Basketball Star who Went on to Coach in Wilkinsburg." *Pittsburgh Post-Gazette*, January 8, 2001.

Pucin, Diane. "Guard from Rider Opening Some Eyes." *Philadelphia Inquirer*, February 8, 1993.

"Rev. Grayson Gives Seven Scholarships to Final Schenley Grads." *New Pittsburgh Courier*, July 8, 2011.

Robbins, Lenn. "St. John's Star Emerges from Rough 'Hood." *New York Post*, December 6, 2009.

Shrum, Rick. "Schenley Boys' Coach Leaves for Butler CCC." *Pittsburgh Post-Gazette*, July 11, 2007.

Simon, Mark. "Shots They'll Never Forget." ESPN.com, December 24, 2003.

Smith, Dean. "Silver Hawks Finish Third in Palms." *Sanford Herald*, December 27, 2006.

Smizik, Bob. "Schenley Slips Past Wilkinsburg." *Pittsburgh Press*, March 9, 1978.

Sostek, Anya. "The Last Class of Schenley Represents Bittersweet Chapter in a Proud History." *Pittsburgh Post-Gazette*, May 29, 2011.

Sullivan, Paul. "Proviso East Lives up to Expectations." *Chicago Tribune*, March 17, 1991.

"Super 25: Virginia's Oak Hill Academy Finishes on Top." *USA Today*, March 27, 2007.

Tarkanian, Jerry and Dan Wetzel. *Runnin' Rebel: Shark Tales of "Extra Benefits," Frank Sinatra, and Winning It All*. Champaign, IL: Sports Publishing, LLC, 2005.

Teltsch, Kathleen. "Reacting to Rising Violence, Schools Introduce 'Fourth R': Reconciliation." *New York Times*, December 26, 1990.

Thamel, Pete. "DeJuan Blair's Backside Provides a Big Upside for Pitt." *New York Times*, March 25, 2009.

White, Mike. "Obituary: Calvin Kane, Jr. Helped Schenley High to 1978 State Championship." *Pittsburgh Post-Gazette*, February 11, 2012.

-----------. "Schenley Cries Foul in Defeat." *Pittsburgh Post-Gazette*, March 25, 2001.

-----------. "Schenley Falls to Erie Prep, 53-49." *Pittsburgh Post-Gazette*, March 13, 2005.

-----------. "Schenley's First-year Starter Kane Shines, Leading the Spartans in a 68-65 Win." *Pittsburgh Post-Gazette*, December 10, 2006.

-----------. "Schenley's Hotshots Bring Down Moon." *Pittsburgh Post-Gazette*, March 18, 2007.

-----------. "Schenley's Sweet Dreams are Crushed." *Pittsburgh Post-Gazette*, March 26, 2006.

-----------. "Schenley Tops Chester, Lands Long-awaited Title Trophy." *Pittsburgh Post-Gazette*, March 25, 2007.

-----------. "Silver Plated: Schenley Coach Says This was His Most Talented Team." *Pittsburgh Post-Gazette*, March 28, 2001.

-----------. "Sun is Setting on Schenley High." *Pittsburgh Post-Gazette*, February 18, 2011.

Wills, Rick. "Final Classes of Langley, Oliver High Schools Graduate." *Pittsburgh Tribune-Review*, June 9, 2012.

Winn, Luke. "Iowa State's DeAndre Kane Making the Most of His Second Chance." *Sports Illustrated*, February 5, 2014.

----------. "The Transfer Study: A Look into Commitment Habits of 700 Top Players." *Sports Illustrated*, August 1, 2013.

"Wizards Extend Longest Winning Streak since 2007." *Associated Press*, April 25, 2012.

Yake, D. Byron. "Schenley, Norristown Battle Tonight for PIAA Basketball Crown." *Associated Press*, March 27, 1971.

Zlatos, Bill. "1 of 3 City Kids Drop out." *Pittsburgh Tribune-Review*, July 13, 2006.

----------. "Close Schenley, Roosevelt Urges." *Pittsburgh Tribune-Review*, May 20, 2008.

----------. "'Ghosts of Past' Plague Closed Schenley High School in North Oakland." *Pittsburgh Tribune-Review*, February 11, 2013.

----------. "Panel Recommends PMC Property Group be Awarded Bid for Schenley High School Sale." *Pittsburgh Tribune-Review*, February 6, 2013.

Acknowledgments

WHAT MAKES YOU SO RIVETED by high school basketball? What makes it more alluring than the NBA, where the world's best players ply their trade? I'm often asked a variation of these fundamental questions by some of the sports fans with whom I come into contact.

I could answer them by explaining my affection for scholastic hoops, extolling the virtues that made me fall in love with the game. But after having read this book, you can see how those virtues are endangered. Instead, I usually frame my response around the countless aspects of the NBA I dislike.

Basketball has always been and will always be my favorite sport, but I am a longstanding member of the small faction of disgruntled fans who can no longer stomach the NBA. (We are clearly a minority, considering how Disney and Time Warner will be paying the league $2.67 billion—yes, billion—a year beginning in 2016 for the rights to broadcast its games.) I prefer the NBA's alternatives, the amateur ranks, where—despite the corrosion from the professional game's money and influence—winning for your high school or college can yield a feeling that even a million dollars couldn't buy.

The NBA season is too long. The shot clock is too short, and it produces too much isolation play. Coaches don't teach; they manage egos. Traveling is legal. And bad teams tank the last third of the season for a draft pick they're not guaranteed to receive.

As I'm writing this, the Philadelphia 76ers are in the midst of watching another season spiral down the drain, as they've intentionally compiled a roster for their 2014-15 campaign that couldn't win the Big Ten. At the end of the previous season, during which the club lost 26 consecutive games en route to a 19-63 finish, team owner Joshua Harris said, "I think the season has been a huge success for us." Considering how athletes, coaches, and front offices operate in a world of scripted answers and doubletalk, Harris's candor is refreshing. But his statement is disturbing. After all, the 76ers—the same franchise that once trotted out Wilt Chamberlain, Julius Erving, Moses Malone, Charles Barkley, and Allen Iverson—hadn't won a single game for a stretch of two months in the winter.

However, nothing sums up my disdain for the NBA more than a fact I recently read about the aforementioned Jalen Rose ($139.1 million) and Mike Bibby ($132.5 million), two players whom, ironically, I enjoyed watching throughout the 1990s and 2000s. Combined, they earned more than a quarter of a billion dollars in their careers. Yet they appeared in exactly zero All-Star games. More importantly, neither one led his team to a championship. They suited up for a total of 11 franchises, which means that 11 different fan bases didn't exactly get a return on their emotional and financial investments. I struggle to comprehend how athletes can cash in like that when they haven't reached the peak of their profession.

As the years pass and my hair recedes and waist expands, I find myself less interested in what happens between the lines of the court and more interested in what happens beyond them. You don't have to be from Pittsburgh or live in Western Pennsylvania to be intrigued by the tale of Schenley High School and its basketball program. At its best, the school represented all that is good about public education and sports in the inner-city. Its closing now represents all that is bad about them.

I thought the account of the 2006-07 Spartans would be a good fit for *SLAM,* since I had contributed a few articles to the magazine and its Web site in the past. The more I learned about the team, though, the more I understood that in order to tell the story properly, I needed to widen my lens. This could not be about a single season. The Spartans were the product of not only their school but their neighborhood. Thus, it became clear early on that this story would exceed the 2,000 words, to which *SLAM* limits its features.

I want to thank all of the people whose time and patience helped this project come to fruition, especially Fred Skrocki, DeJuan and Greg Blair, D.J. Kennedy, DeAndre Kane, and Jamaal Bryant. These men have vivid memories of their days at Schenley, and the crown they finally captured means the world to them. I appreciate you sharing the details of your experience with me. I'll never forget the look on each of your faces that evening in March 2007 as you cradled the championship trophy as if it were your long-lost child.

Thank you to Sonny Vaccaro, Charlie Batch, David Kennedy Sr., Sam Clancy, Larry Anderson, Darrick Suber, Nate Gerwig, Kevin Reid, Gregg Downer, Ryan Brooks, Bob Starkman, and numerous others who were generous in answering all of my questions.

I also want to express my gratitude to the dedicated staff, both past and present, at the *Pittsburgh Post-Gazette* and *Pittsburgh Tribune-Review.* Your work has always been informative and creative, and it greatly enhanced the pages of this book. The *Post-Gazette's* Mike White, the dean of scholastic sports in Western Pennsylvania, deserves a special thank-you. His famed career began a year before I was even born, and his reportage was critical to this story. As I was researching your treasure trove of articles, I quickly realized that it would take years for someone to read every word you've written.

Thank you to Eric Hartline, my former colleague at the *Delaware County Daily Times*, whose photography skills are second to none. A nonfiction book is less spellbinding without the art illustrating the narrative and putting faces to names. I also want to thank Pete Curran, an expert on graphic design who took my ideas for the cover and made them look twice as good on the page.

A quick shout-out goes to the men and women who work in the sports-information departments at the different colleges attended by Schenley's stars. Pitt's Greg Hotchkiss, Iowa State's Matthew Shoultz, Mekale Jackson of St. John's, Cincinnati's Ryan Koslen, UNLV's Andy Grossman, Marquette's Maggie Bean, Jacksonville's Alex Keil, La Salle's Kevin Bonner, New Mexico's Matthew Ensor, Rider's Bud Focht, Kent State's Jay Fiorello, and Marshall's Jason Corriher accommodated all of my requests.

Of course, the most credit is reserved for my loving family. My parents Jim and Kathy, brother Matt, and sister Beth have been there for me throughout all the days of my life. And with my wife Allison and son Holden, that life is better than I ever thought it could be. Finally, I want to thank Mya Hostutler, my 7-year-old niece, who is the very personification of strength and courage. Knowing that nothing can conquer your spirit puts a smile on my face.